THE
WORLD
OF
ISAK
DINESEN

seattle • 1961

UNIVERSITY OF WASHINGTON PRESS

THE
WORLD
OF
ISAK
DINESEN

By

Eric O. Johannesson

PREFACE

IN THIS study I have sought to describe the neat and orderly structure which is the world of Isak Dinesen. The material presented has been derived almost exclusively from a close reading of the tales, from a careful scrutiny of characters, plot, setting, and world view.

I have also sought to define what I believe to be the underlying theme of Dinesen's tales: the defense of the story and the art of storytelling, a theme so pervasive that it has come to form the very basis of the author's world view.

I have not felt it in my power to deal with the fascinating personality of Isak Dinesen herself. This pleasant task I have left for bolder investigators.

It is understandable that most of the critics and scholars who have written about Isak Dinesen in the past have devoted their attention primarily to the histrionic figure of Isak Dinesen herself. A few valuable studies of various aspects of Dinesen's art and world have appeared, however, and I should like to acknowledge my indebtedness to some of them, in particular to the perceptive essays of Aage Henriksen, Jørgen Gustava Brandt, and Johannes Rosendahl, from which I have derived much insight. I have also benefited from some of the analyses of Dinesen's tales in Hans Brix's *Karen Blixens Eventyr*. Christian Elling's brilliant essay "Karen Blixen" in *Danske Digtere i det Tyvende Aarhundrede* has been most instrumental in helping to form my own view of Dinesen's world.

In order not to burden the study with too many footnotes, I have indicated the sources of textual references in parentheses. This has necessitated the use of a few abbreviations which are to be understood as follows: SGT refers to *Seven Gothic Tales*, WT to *Winter's Tales*, LT to *Last Tales*, AD to *Anecdotes of Destiny*, and OA to *Out of Africa*.

Grateful acknowledgments are due to many of my teachers and colleagues at the University of California in Berkeley, especially to Assar G. Janzén, Professor of Scandinavian and former chairman of the department, without whose energetic support of Scandinavian studies in the United States and unfailing personal encouragement this essay would never have been written; and to Professors Håkon Hamre, Andrew O. Jászi, and Børge Gedsø Madsen for their friendly interest and assistance during my years of graduate study.

ERIC O. JOHANNESSON

CONTENTS

THE
WORLD
OF
ISAK
DINESEN

INTRODUCTION

I N 1934 A BOOK entitled *Seven Gothic Tales* caused considerable excitement in the literary world. A collection of rather bizarre tales, which soon became a best seller and is now a recognized classic, it was the work of an unknown author described, in the words of Dorothy Canfield, as "a Continental European, writing in English although that is not native to his pen, who wishes his-or-her identity not to be known." [1]

The author was soon unmasked. Isak Dinesen turned out to be the nom de plume of the Danish Baroness Karen Blixen-Finecke.

The job of unmasking was not too difficult, for in choosing the pseudonym Dinesen, the author had merely used her own maiden name.

The name Dinesen was already familiar to most Danish readers, because Isak Dinesen's father, Captain Wilhelm Dinesen, also known by the pseudonym Boganis, is the author of a series of *Jagtbreve* (*Letters from the Hunt*), which have become classical within their genre.

3

The Dinesen family is an old Danish family with firmly rooted aristocratic traditions. The author's great-grandfather, Jens Kraft Dinesen (1768-1827), was the owner of a large estate, Kragerup, in Western Sealand. After his death one of the sons inherited Kragerup, while another son, Adolph Wilhelm Dinesen, the author's grandfather, bought an estate called Katholm in 1839. A colorful and heroic figure, he once accompanied H. C. Andersen during the latter's Roman journey, volunteered for the French Army in Algeria in 1837, became a major, and won considerable fame.[2]

Captain Wilhelm Dinesen, the author's father, followed in his father's footsteps. He won distinction in the field, first at the battle of Dybbøl during the Dano-Prussian War, later on the side of the French in the Franco-Prussian War. In the 1870's he went to the United States and lived for a couple of years among the Indians in Wisconsin. After his return to Denmark, he settled at Rungstedlund, situated on the coast halfway between Copenhagen and Elsinore. Here Isak Dinesen was born in 1885. She still resides in the yellow eighteenth-century building, which once was an inn and the home of the Danish poet Johannes Ewald.

Isak Dinesen did not have plans to become a writer like her father, though she published a few Gothic tales in a leading Danish periodical as early as 1908-9. At the time she used the pseudonym Osceola. She was interested in art and studied painting. Africa changed her mind.

It was shortly before the first World War that Dinesen went to Africa, where she managed a large coffee plantation in Kenya in British East Africa for some eighteen years. In 1931 falling prices and a series of bad harvests forced her to sell the farm and return to Denmark. Her marriage, in 1914, to the Swedish Baron Bror Blixen-Finecke, a big-game hunter and sportsman, ended in divorce in 1921. The loss of the farm

4

was a severe blow to Isak Dinesen, but it made her into a writer. In order to alleviate her sorrow at having to leave the African world which she had learned to love, the place where she had felt at home, and in order to forget her daily troubles, she began to write stories. "If I had kept the farm," she says, "I would never have become a writer." [3]

The years in Africa also made Isak Dinesen into an English writer since English was the language she used almost daily for twenty years. She still writes in English, sometimes translating the English text into Danish herself.

In Denmark the initial critical reception of the *Seven Gothic Tales* was not too favorable. In the 1930's Danish literature was predominantly sociological and psychological, and the tales of Dinesen appeared rather strange and foreign to the critics.

The picture changed a few years later, in 1937, with the publication of *Out of Africa*, Dinesen's reminiscences about her years in Kenya, written in order to preserve her memory of Africa, its landscape, its fauna, its people. It is considered by many to be Dinesen's finest work, and the critics spoke favorably of its warmly human tone. *Winter's Tales* in 1942 was also very well received.

In 1944 the Danish reading public was mystified by the appearance of a novel of adventure entitled *Gengaeldelsens Veje* (in English in 1947 as *The Angelic Avengers*), supposedly the work of a French writer by the name Pierre Andrézel. The novel became quite popular and inspired Professor Hans Brix, the eminent Danish scholar, to carry out a magnificent piece of detective work, in which he tried to prove by stylistic analysis that Pierre Andrézel was but another pseudonym for Karen Blixen. [4] A few years ago the mystery was solved when Karen Blixen admitted in an interview that she was, in fact, the author of the novel, which she insisted she had written as a mere entertainment.[5]

Few critics had been as perceptive as Tom Kristensen when he wrote in 1935 that at the heart of Dinesen's tales was an original view of life based on personal experience.[6] The truth of Kristensen's remarks became more and more evident as Isak Dinesen continued to publish her exotic and entertaining stories. Thus her position in Danish letters changed radically: from having been thought of as an anachronism in the 1930's, she developed into the leading figure of Danish literary life in the 1950's. The first Danish writer since H. C. Andersen and Søren Kierkegaard to receive worldwide recognition, she has been suggested as a candidate for the Nobel Prize, and showered with honors. Dinesen's recent collections of tales, *Last Tales* (1957) and *Anecdotes of Destiny* (1958), testify to a creative ability undiminished after a long illness.

Literary historians and critics in Scandinavia have made much of Dinesen's uniqueness. There is undoubtedly some truth to their assertions. Though it is not difficult to discover superficial affinities between the tales of Dinesen and the tales of, say, Carson McCullers, or Somerset Maugham, just as it is not difficult to detect superficial resemblances to the tales of older writers, say, Thomas Mann, or Joseph Conrad, or Robert Louis Stevenson, or Guy de Maupassant, or Barbey d'Aurevilly, because Dinesen is an expert in the art of pastiche, nevertheless her art and her vision of life are of such striking originality that she is not to be likened to any one of these writers.

The literary historians have, for this reason, encountered some difficulty in finding a niche for Isak Dinesen in the history of contemporary Scandinavian literature.[7] Still, it is possible that a comparison between Dinesen and an older Scandinavian writer might serve to throw some light on this problem. Though there are considerable differences between the two writers, the Swedish novelist and storyteller Selma Lagerlöf (1858-1940) and Isak Dinesen have a lot in common.

Like Isak Dinesen, Selma Lagerlöf made her appearance on the literary scene at a time when naturalism was the dominant mode of expression in Scandinavia. In 1891 *Gösta Berlings Saga* became a success because it appeared at a time when naturalistic writers such as Strindberg and Ibsen had begun to feel the need for myth, and when storytelling had been subordinated to psychological or sociological analysis.[8] *Gösta Berlings Saga* marked the return to myth and storytelling. The novel consisted primarily of a series of tales loosely strung together, and showed clearly that the author was relying heavily on the oral tradition of storytelling.

When *Seven Gothic Tales* appeared Sven Møller Kristensen spoke of it as "something isolated and foreign, like an element from another world, in the critical and sociological Danish literature of the thirties." [9] In retrospect, it seems to mark the beginning of a strong antinaturalistic trend, later to be supported by the works of Martin A. Hansen and H. C. Branner. Thus the *Seven Gothic Tales,* like *Gösta Berlings Saga* some forty years earlier, marked the return to myth and storytelling. Based as they were on the oral tradition of storytelling, on classical motifs, on fairy tales and myths, the tales of Dinesen met with a ready response from a generation feeling "a need for myth." [10] They have undoubtedly been a great influence on the younger generation of writers in Scandinavia, who are once again, like the writers of the 1890's, manifesting a tendency toward romanticism and storytelling, and a desire to liberate the imagination from the fetters of naturalism.[11]

With Isak Dinesen the story has once again regained its supremacy within the art of fiction.

1
THE

ART OF
THE STORY

A Modern Scheherazade

I HAVE always thought that I would have cut a figure at the time of the plague of Florence." This quotation from *Out of Africa* (p. 225) suggests the kind of role that Isak Dinesen has conceived for herself. Like Selma Lagerlöf, who liked to regard her audience as children listening to stories, Isak Dinesen has always imagined herself in the classic role of the storyteller, as a modern Scheherazade. Her tales are so imbued with the spirit of storytelling that one might venture to assert that the basic theme running through them all is, in fact, the storyteller's defense of the art of the story.

It was evidently the long droughts of Africa that made Dinesen into a storyteller. Because she felt the need of collecting her energy, she began, she says, "in the evening to write stories, fairy-tales and romances, that would take my mind a long way off, to other countries and times." These were stories that she had previously told to her friends, particularly to Denys Finch-Hatton, for

8

Denys, says Dinesen, "had a trait of character which to me was very precious, he liked to hear a story told" (OA, p. 225).

The storyteller needs an audience, and in this respect Dinesen was fortunate. In Africa she found eager listeners among the natives. While the art of listening to stories has been lost in Europe, Dinesen maintains, "the Natives of Africa, who cannot read, have still got it; if you begin to them: 'There was a man who walked out on the plain and there he met another man,' you have them all with you, their minds running upon the unknown track of the men on the plain" (OA, pp. 225-26). Together, her friends and the natives must have encouraged Dinesen's faith in the story, in "something you can tell. Like one can *tell Ali Baba and the Forty Thieves* but one could never *tell Anna Karenina.*"[1]

The reference to the *Arabian Nights* is not without significance. The stories that make up this immortal collection are, as Dinesen suggests, dependent on the oral tradition of storytelling, they are tales to be told. Moreover, they are told with a specific purpose: they are told in order to change the morbid mind and cold heart of the King. In accomplishing this purpose, they also indirectly proclaim the power of the story.

It is, as Hans Brix has said, difficult to trace with certainty specific influences on Dinesen's tales because her heritage as storyteller is so vast and varied.[2] She is, as she puts it, three thousand years old because she is telling the old tales over again. The stories of the Bible, the Norse sagas, the *Odyssey,* the classic collections of folk tales: they have all stimulated her imagination and influenced her manner of storytelling.

Still, if one were to single out the work that has meant the most to Isak Dinesen, it would undoubtedly be the *Arabian Nights.* Dinesen's tales are replete with allusions to this book, and she often employs the exotic Orient as the setting for her tales. Haroun al Raschid is often referred to: his habit of masquerading has appealed to the imagination of a writer who loves to cultivate this histrionic habit. The philosophy of Islam with its emphasis on acceptance seems to have influenced Dinesen profoundly. In Africa, on the farm, the people about her must have seemed like some of the figures in the *Arabian Nights,* and their attitudes to life, for which she expresses great understanding, like those of faithful Mohammedans.

The stories in the *Arabian Nights* are arabesques in the true sense of the word. They are intricate stories woven around interlaced tales. Many of Dinesen's tales resemble such arabesques, intricate embroideries with stories within the story. The Gothic tales, in particular, belong to this type.

As already mentioned, the stories in the *Arabian Nights* are told with a specific purpose in mind. The young Scheherazade is telling her stories in order to save her own life, and in order to change the heart and mind of the King. The King is presented with a human comedy which brings him a new vision of life. "Apprehending the grave and constant in human experience simultaneously with the ridiculous and ephemeral," says Joseph Campbell, "he saw his own fate, finally, in perspective, and abandoning his Hamlet act, rejoined the race." But in order to provide this epiphany Scheherazade was forced, as Campbell puts it, to create "a universe of story; or rather, the universe *as* story," a world in which "no sober stone is permitted to kill even the wildest fancy, yet unlikelihood becomes an epiphany of humanity."[3]

Dinesen's tales, like the stories in the *Arabian Nights,* proclaim the belief in the all but magic power of the story to provide man with a new vision and a renewed faith in life. Her figures are often Hamlet figures, melancholy young men or women who wait for fate to lend them a helping hand, who wait for the storyteller to provide them with a destiny by placing them in a story, or by telling them a story. The degree of probability or improbability of the tale is of little consequence, for in a world transformed by fantasy all is possible.

While the influence of the *Arabian Nights* on the art of Isak Dinesen seems the most profound and far-reaching, there are undoubtedly many other works of art that have left their marks on her mode of storytelling. The Book of Job, the *Decameron*, the comedies of Shakespeare, the tales of Voltaire and E. T. A. Hoffmann, of Alfred de Vigny and Barbey d'Aurevilly, the novels and tales of Walter Scott, Stendhal, Robert Louis Stevenson, Selma Lagerlöf, and Joseph Conrad: all of these, and many others, have probably influenced the art of Dinesen in one way or another.[4] Her tales are a veritable gold mine for students of comparative literature.

Among the writers of the works listed above some are novelists, but most of them are, primarily, writers of tales. The names that are conspicuously absent are those of the creators of the modern psychological novel, the novel that cannot be *told*. In Dinesen's conception of fiction the story and the psychological novel are at opposite poles.

The Story and the Novel

In several of the *Last Tales* Isak Dinesen has, contrary to her practice, made some very explicit and significant comments about her own art. Embedded in these tales is an eloquent defense of the story, of romance.

In one of these, "The Cardinal's First Tale," a lady who has just been listening to Cardinal Salviati's story of his life remarks:

> Your Eminence, in answer to a question, has been telling me a story, in which my friend and teacher is the hero. I see the hero of the story very clearly, as if luminous even, and on a higher

plane. But my teacher and adviser—and my friend—is farther away than before. He no more looks to me quite human, and alas, I am not sure that I am not afraid of him [LT, p. 23].

The Cardinal feels "that is all in the order of things," but adds:

> I see, today, a new art of narration, a novel literature and category of belles-lettres, dawning upon the world. It is indeed, already with us, and it has gained great favor amongst the readers of our time. And this new art and literature—for the sake of the individual characters in the story, and in order to keep close to them and not be afraid—will be ready to sacrifice the story itself [LT, p. 23].

The Cardinal then goes on to praise the novel as "a noble art, a great, earnest and ambitious human product." "But," he continues, "it is a human product. The divine art is the story. In the beginning was the story" (LT, p. 24).

He further maintains that "a story has a hero to it," while "by the time when the new literature shall reign supreme you will have no more stories, you will have no more heroes." "The world," he says, "will have to do without them, sadly, until the hour when divine powers shall see fit, once more, to make a story for a hero to appear in" (LT, p. 24). The disappearance of the story is followed by the disappearance of the heroine, the hero's prize and reward: "By the time when you have no more stories," says the Cardinal, "your young women will be the prize and reward of nobody and nothing. Indeed, I doubt whether by then you will have any young women at all." The hero will "see his lady disrobed of her story or her epos and, all naked, turned into an individual" (LT, p. 25).

The story, the divine art, is different. "The story," says the Cardinal, "according to its essence and plan, moves and places these two young people, hero and heroine,—together with their confidants and competitors, friends, foes and fools

—and goes on." The story provides for the hero and for the heroine but "does not slacken its speed to occupy itself with the mien or bearing of its characters, but goes on" toward its "promised end" (LT, p. 25).

The latter remark occasions the lady to remonstrate against this approach to storytelling. "What you call the divine art," she tells the Cardinal, "to me seems a hard and cruel game, which maltreats and mocks its human beings." To which the Cardinal makes this reply:

> Hard and cruel it may seem, yet we, who hold our high office as keepers and watchmen to the story, may tell you, verily, that to its human characters there is salvation in nothing else in the universe. If you tell them—you compassionate and accommodating human readers—that they may bring their distress and anguish before any other authority, you will be cruelly deceiving and mocking them. For within our whole universe the story only has authority to answer that cry of heart of its characters, that one cry of heart of each of them: *"Who am I?"* [LT, pp. 25-26].

This eloquent dialogue in defense of the story presents an interesting argument. Most readers, like the lady, would probably disagree with the Cardinal's point of view, arguing that the modern psychological novel, which seeks to give the illusion of the very flow of the human consciousness, brings us closer to a definition of character. Still, an eminent critic such as Lionel Trilling seems to feel that the Cardinal's argument is quite valid. In a recent essay Trilling compares Dinesen's *Last Tales* and James Agee's psychological novel *A Death in the Family* and comments with regard to the dialogue in "The Cardinal's First Tale": "The less concerned with story we have become, and the more concerned we are with characters and with understanding them, the less we have been able to perceive and conceive character," and goes on to add: "It is where the story asserts itself, where the novel most frankly allies itself with what Henry James called 'romance' that character is most memorable." Speaking of some of these heroes of romance, a Julien Sorel, a Leatherstocking, a Captain Ahab, Trilling continues: "Like the remembered heroes of the famous old stories, they are known to us not through their traits but through their fates—it is less true to say of them that their characters are their fates than that their fates are their characters." [5]

In the story fate is character: the story moves the hero and the heroine and their attendants toward the "promised end," the moment when they discover the answer to their quest for identity. The storyteller is responsible for his characters, for he is the authority before whom they "may bring their distress and anguish." The storyteller must provide a destiny for his hero or his heroine, and he does this by putting them into a story. The greatest happiness from the hero's point of view is to become part of a story. Many of Dinesen's characters express their delight at having finally entered into a story.

In "The Diver" the "happy" man listening to the poet's story about Saufe, the theology student who once tried to make himself a pair of wings in order to be like the angels, turns out to be that same Saufe. Having heard the poet's story, he says:

> Once I had the welfare of the Softa Saufe, of whom you have just told me, much at heart. By this time I had almost forgotten him. But I am pleased to know that he has got into a story, for that is probably what he was made for, and in future I shall leave him therein confidently. Go on with your tale, Mira Jama, story-teller, and let me hear the end of it [AD, p. 15].

Whether the stories are true or not does not matter in the least, which is fortunate, since Dinesen's stories are, in the words of Trilling, "all lies. Their matter is magic and witchcraft, infants exchanged at birth, brothers and sisters who marry unknown to each other, beautiful giantesses, undying passions,—suchlike nonsense." The tales are told, as Trilling says, "with an air that leads us to believe that they are involved with truth of a kind not available to minds that submit to strict veracity." [6] Dinesen's stories are often contrived and improbable, but in the skillful hands of the storyteller the characters are brought to their appointed end, to the moment of insight.

Some readers undoubtedly feel, like the compassionate lady in "The Cardinal's First Tale," that Dinesen's approach to storytelling is "a hard and cruel game" because it reduces the characters, the human beings in the story, to marionettes, to puppets moved by "divine powers" and their representative, the storyteller, "the keeper and watchman to the story." In Dinesen's tales life itself becomes a marionette comedy, and the figures appear like such marionettes.

Marionettes

One of the remarkable features of Dinesen's style is the use of images, and one of the most common types suggests a mechanical or artificial behavior or being.

In "The Deluge at Norderney" the movements of the four central figures in the boat are compared to those of "four marionettes pulled by the same wire" (SGT, p. 13). Calypso von Platen-Hallermund finds her uncle asleep in his bed, only "a poor little doll stuffed with sawdust, a caricature of a skull" (SGT, p. 49).

In "The Old Chevalier" Baron von Brackel thinks of the husband of his former mistress as "the gigantic shadow, upon the white back-curtain, of an absurd little punchinello" (SGT, p. 85). Nathalie is compared to a doll (SGT, p. 92; p. 93), and the Baron thinks that "her bright painted cheeks looked even more like a doll's above her fair naked body" (SGT, p. 98).

In "The Monkey" Boris sees himself in his mind, "in his white uniform, as a marionette, pulled alternately by the deadly determined old lady and the deadly determined young lady" (SGT, p. 138).

In "The Roads Round Pisa" the old major-domo getting out of the carriage is said to look like Pantalone (SGT, p. 178). As Agnese tells her story the rest of the participants stand "perfectly immobile, like a party of little wooden dolls placed on that terrace of the inn, in the middle of the great landscape" (SGT, p. 205). Giovanni and Agnese are compared to "the marionettes of the night before," because "they were within stronger hands than their own, and had no idea what was going to happen to them" (SGT, p. 209).

In "The Supper at Elsinore" the people on the icy sound look "like little rows of small black tin soldiers upon the infinite gray plane" (SGT, p. 232). The Bishop appears ridiculously small, "like a little doll seen from a tower" (SGT, p. 257).

In "The Poet" the King is likened to "an elegant, powdered and corseted little doll with a blank face" (SGT, p. 359). The young dancer at La Liberté looks like a doll:

> . . . not like the dolls of the present day, which are imitations of the faces and forms of human babies, but like the dolls of old days which strove, parallel with humanity, toward an abstract ideal of feminine beauty. Her big eyes were clear as glass, and her long eyelashes and delicate eyebrows were as black as if they had been painted on her face [SGT, p. 368].

She had the "placid, happy face of a doll" (SGT, p. 375). As the Councilor lies dying he refers to Fransine and Anders as "sacred puppets" (SGT, p. 419).

Mizzi in "The Invincible Slaveowners" has "a curious likeness to a doll," and inspires "in onlookers the sentiment of humorous tenderness with which one looks at a big, beautiful doll" (WT, p. 129).

In "Copenhagen Season" the old ladies have been rendered "small and light as dolls" by the years (LT, p. 269).

Some of these doll or marionette images refer to specific actions of the figures as being doll-like or mechanical. Sometimes they suggest that the figures are acting in some sort of marionette comedy.

When Miss Nat-og-Dag in "The Deluge at Norderney" looks at her maid her glance is the sort "by which you judge whether a person is likely to make a satisfactory fourth at a game of cards" (SGT, p. 12). The Cardinal feels that the Lord might "be about to play a fine game with us" (SCT, p. 15).

In "The Dreamers" ballet images are very common. When Baron Guildenstern relates his adventure with Rosalba he speaks of their relationship as a *pas-de-deux*: "She and I . . . were as much in contact as if we had been performing a *pas-de-deux* upon the center of a stage, with the aged *corps du ballet* grouped around us" (SGT, p. 307). And again: Rosalba "seemed to like me, but in amorous *pas-de-deux* she was slow of movement." When Lincoln Forsner pursues Pellegrina in the Alps, he feels that he is in "a maddening situation, suitable for an extravaganza for the theaters of Rome" (SGT, p. 320).

In "The Cardinal's First Tale" Salviati tells of his mother's life in the palace as "a majestic and graceful regatta, with streamers flying" (LT, p. 17). Like her husband she leads a life that is pure theater:

> In the course of time the old Prince completed his role on the stage of life, draped his grandeur and loneliness round him in heavy

17

folds of black marble, and lay down to rest in the mausoleum, at Dionysio's side. Even that fair lady, the Princess Benedetta, like to a child at eventide, yawned and let go of her dolls [LT, p. 20].

In "A Country Tale" Eitel sees himself and Ulrikke talking of their disaster "as if it had been the tragedy of a hero and a heroine in a book" (LT, p. 201).

Ballet images are common in "Converse at Night." In their happy intoxication a certain rhythm appears to force the King and Yorick apart "as when two dancers in a ballet separate, and the one, although still close at hand and indispensable to the figure, remains inactive, observing his partner's great solo" (LT, p. 333). After a long speech Yorick comes back "to his partner in the dance, and in front of the latter's figure, which had remained immovable on the spot, he made ready for their *pas-de-deux*" (LT, p. 334). The King receives him "gracefully and harmoniously as a dancer" (LT, p. 334). Later he makes one "last, flying, completely weightless leap—as in the language of the ballet is called *grand jeté*," before he finishes his last oratorical solo (LT, p. 339).

In a number of cases similes and metaphors are used which because of their military origin suggest a certain mechanical or artificial behavior.

In "The Monkey" Athena "[swells] over a little in her feeling of invincibility, like a young captain advancing into fire, with a high courage, overbearingly" (SGT, p. 140). In the seduction scene her posture is "that of a warrior, clinging to the hilt of his lifted sword, taking a vital vow" (SGT, p. 154). Athena's world is "tumbling down to the right and left of her, like a position under heavy gun fire" (SGT, p. 158).

In "The Supper at Elsinore" the two sisters move "like two grenadiers at parade" (SGT, p. 247).

At Cocoza's command, *"En scène pour le deux,"* Pellegrina

in "The Dreamers" responds "like a soldier to the call, or a war horse to the blast of the trumpet" (SGT, p. 352).

In "The Invincible Slaveowners" Mizzi rises "like a soldier on parade" (WT, p. 132).

If Dinesen's human figures are described as if they were marionettes, they are also treated like marionettes. They become involved in patterns of events so fantastic that they are not able to grasp the significance of these events while they are taking place. However, in the end they are rewarded, they are rewarded with an insight into their problems. Thus it would not be correct to argue that they are reduced to being mere marionettes. Paradoxically enough, their marionette status lifts them to a higher plane. Dinesen's tales tend, in fact, to become epiphanies because they concentrate on the turning point in human experience, the moment when the truth is revealed and we see in a flash the pattern of meaning. Though they are often as fantastic and as improbable as the intrigues of opera librettos, these tales do bring this epiphany to the characters.

Epiphanies

A few years ago W. H. Auden published some reflections on opera and drama which seem particularly relevant in this context.[7] "The librettist," says Auden,

> need never bother his head, as the dramatist must, about probability. A credible situation in opera means a situation in which it is credible that someone should sing. A good libretto plot is a melodrama in both the strict and the conventional sense of the word; it offers as many opportunities as possible for the characters to be swept off their feet by placing them in situations which are too tragic or too fantastic for "words" [pp. 15-16].

This statement seems very relevant here. In Dinesen's tales

a credible situation is, I think, a situation in which it is credible that someone should tell a story. The plot seems often but a reason for getting some people together so that they can tell stories.

Auden continues with the remark that the golden age of opera, from Mozart to Verdi, "coincided with the golden age of liberal humanism, of unquestioning belief in freedom and progress." Since we no longer live in such an age some have hazarded the opinion that operas are impossible. Auden disagrees: "That would only follow," he says, "if we should cease to believe in free will and personality altogether. Every high C accurately struck demolishes the theory that we are the irresponsible puppets of fate or chance" (p. 18). This seems again a statement very applicable to Dinesen's tales. Dinesen's figures often appear as mere puppets because they serve the plot, but through the story they attain to new levels of awareness, to a mating with destiny, which indicates, precisely, that they are not irresponsible puppets of fate or chance. To the high C of the opera corresponds the moment of vision or insight in the tales.

With very few exceptions Dinesen's plots serve exactly this function: they are designed to provide a central figure, or several figures, with a new vision or insight. A glance at the various tales reveals that most of them have a specific relevance to the predicament of a central observer who is himself sometimes implicated in the action. The tale as a whole, or the part of it told to him, is designed to provide him with a new vision of life. This explains, incidentally, why so many of Dinesen's central characters are melancholy dreamers, observers of life, who wait for destiny to provide them with a sign. The melancholy hero as such does not necessarily interest Isak Dinesen: she needs a melancholy figure as a focus because he is by his very nature waiting to receive an insight of some kind.

He is waiting for the storyteller to move him. A few examples will illustrate this.

In one of the *Winter's Tales,* "A Consolatory Tale," the central figure is the writer Charlie Despard. As the story begins he is sitting in a café in Paris. He is in a state of utter despair, and feels that it is a curse to be a writer. His friend Aeneas arrives. During the course of the evening, the latter tells Charlie a story, "a consolatory tale," which makes him see his position as a writer in a new light. He has been given a valuable insight into life, and he will go on writing.

"The Young Man with the Carnation" is also a story about Charlie Despard. He is in a state of despair over his writing ability, and the mistake he commits in sleeping in someone else's bedroom with someone else's mistress is like a sign from God that he should not despair. When he realizes his mistake and goes over the details of the nights before, "with the experienced eye of an author of fiction, they moved him as mightily as if they had been out of one of his own books. . . . 'Almighty God,' he said from the bottom of his heart, 'as the heavens are higher than the earth, so are thy short stories higher than our short stories'" (WT, p. 23). There is an expression of rapture, laughter, and delight in his face. A light has fallen upon him, and "it seemed that he was to see himself, within it, as God saw him, and under this test he had to steady himself by the table" (WT, p. 24). The mistake has brought him a new insight into his own life, and into his condition as an artist.

In "The Roads Round Pisa" a young Dane "of melancholy disposition," Augustus von Schimmelmann, is waiting for a sign. Brooding about the truth of his life, he wonders: "But what will happen to me now? I do not know what to do with myself or my life. Can I trust to fate to hold out a helping hand to me just for once?" And he thinks of the little smelling bottle he carries in his pocket, once given to a maiden aunt of his when she was traveling in Italy (SGT, p. 167). At the end of the tale he is given an identical smelling bottle by the old Lady Carlotta, and he feels that there is in this coincidence, "in this decision of fate, something which was meant for him only—a value, a depth, a resort even, in life which belonged to him alone, and which he could not share with anybody else any more than he would be able to share his dreams" (SGT, p. 216). His role in the marionette comedy of life has been determined. His reward for being a good marionette is—a smelling bottle.

Even the other figures in the tale come to a realization of some sort. Lady Carlotta realizes that

> . . . life is a mosaic work of the Lord's, which he keeps filling in bit by bit. If I had seen this little bit of bright color as the center-piece, I would have understood the pattern, and would not have shaken it all to pieces so many times, and given the good Lord so much trouble in putting it together again [SGT, p. 215].

The old Prince Pozentiani realizes that "we fail because we are too small." "Too small I have been," he says, "too small for the ways of God" (SGT, p. 207).

In "Sorrow Acre" the events bring to Adam a new aware-ness of his own destiny and a deeper understanding of life. The events of the day bring to him "a deeper sense of pity with all that lived than he had ever known" (WT, p. 48). Later, "his pity with all creation" comes to include the uncle, too. Then he suddenly sees "the ways of life . . . as a twined and tangled design, complicated and mazy," and realizes that "it was not given him or any mortal to command or control it. Life and death, happiness and woe, the past and the present, were interlaced within the pattern" (WT, p. 60). He realizes that all that lives must suffer, and he becomes aware of the unity of all things, "the secret which connects the phenomena of existence" (WT, p. 61). He feels that "this hour was consecrated to greater emotions, to a surrender to fate and to the will of life" (WT, p. 62).

In "Alkmene" the young squire Vilhelm comes to realize that "the forces amongst which I had been moving were mightier and more formidable than I had guessed, and that my whole world might be about to sink under me" (WT, p. 217). The parson, too, seems to have had "a sudden and splendid revelation" on his deathbed, having cried out "that now he understood the ways of the Lord" (WT, p. 215).

Emilie Vandamm in "The Dreaming Child" is also given a deeper understanding of life through a child, the dreamer Jens. She comes to realize that the boy was her own child, her and Charlie Dreyer's son. After the death of Jens she understands everything: "there is a grace in the world, such as none of us know about. The world is not a hard or severe place, as people tell us. It is not even just. You are forgiven everything. The fine things of the world you cannot wrong or harm. They are much too strong for that." She feels "the generosity of the world" (WT, pp. 186-87).

To Jensine in "The Pearl" the added pearl brings a new insight, a realization that she will never conquer "these people, who know neither care nor fear. It is as in the Bible; I shall bruise their heel, but they shall bruise my head" (WT, p. 123).

In "The Old Chevalier" Baron von Brackel tells his tale to his young friend in order to illustrate a theme, recurrent in the literature of the past, which they were discussing: "namely, whether one is ever likely to get any real benefit, any lasting moral satisfaction, out of forsaking an inclination for the sake of principle" (SGT, p. 81).

At the end of "The Heroine" Frederick Lamond is provided

with "such a vision of life, and of the world" as none of the faces which the great masters paint had ever given him (WT, p. 88).

Through the experience with Mizzi, Axel Leth in "The Invincible Slaveowners" comes to feel himself to be "the instrument of destiny," and arrives at the realization that "the slave-owner's dependency upon the slave is strong as death and as cruel as the grave" (WT, pp. 146-47).

Lady Flora Gordon in "The Cardinal's Third Tale" hurls her challenge against the gods and is given an answer, a sign. The syphilitic wound on her lip is like a rose and a seal, and brings her a new and deep sense of humility and understanding.

The list of names could be enlarged, but these examples should suffice to illustrate the point: the majority of the tales are designed to provide a central observer with a new insight into life. These insights are of various kinds. Some figures are brought to realize the unity and interdependence of all things. Others are brought to a realization of the greatness and scope of God's imagination, and an acceptance of the fact that we are only marionettes in God's great marionette comedy. Others learn that the condition of man must be accepted as it is, though it is fraught with injustice and suffering, for God is just, and God is great. Others attain a vision of life as a noble and elevated game in which the players must obey the rules, though it entails paying a high price.

Thus Dinesen moves her figures to their appointed end. They are treated like dolls, like marionettes, but they reach a new awareness, experience a moment of recognition.

One might argue, at this point, that it is in the nature of the short story as such to concentrate on a turning point in experience, and that there is nothing unique about Dinesen's method.

There is a difference, however. If we consider, for a moment, the tales of Joseph Conrad, the difference becomes quite apparent. In the tales of Conrad the action moves inexorably toward the moment of recognition, and the crisis occurs, as Morton Dauwen Zabel says, "when, by a stroke of accident, or by an act of decision or error rising from the secret necessities of temperament, a man finds himself abruptly committed to his destiny." The moment of recognition is "the stroke by which fate compels recognition—of one's self, of reality, of illusion, error, mistaken expectation, and defeat." [8] Character is fate.

In Dinesen's tales, on the other hand, very little of what happens to a man has to do with his character, with "the secret necessities of temperament." The moment of recognition is compelled by fate. When the hero recognizes that his imagination has not been sufficient to fathom the workings of destiny, he does not regard the events which have taken place as motivated by his own nature. Unlike Conrad's heroes, who indulge, as Zabel puts it, in "long recitatives, monologues, and self-inquisitions," Dinesen's figures lack insight into their own nature: they are waiting for destiny to mold it. [9] Thus fate comes to determine their character, providing them not only with an answer to the question "Who am I?" but also with a recognition of the nature of reality.

The Oral Tradition

In treating her figures as marionettes, and in letting them discover their identities, their characters, through their fates, Dinesen has clearly revealed her dependence on the oral tradition of storytelling and romance. Her tales are, as Trilling says, "always *told* rather than written." [10] But the characteristic qualities of Dinesen's tales are by no means peculiar to her

mode of expression: they are the characteristic qualities of
the tale as a literary genre.

Oral storytelling requires a narrator. Such a narrator is often
present in Dinesen's tales. Very often a tale contains stories
within the story: the characters are telling each other stories.
In some other cases the narrator is absent, but in such instances
we are, I suppose, to look upon Isak Dinesen herself as the
storyteller, masquerading for Karen Blixen.

The narrator's language is highly mannered, and yet very
simple, direct, and concrete. Abstract reflections are rare because the storyteller *thinks* in stories. As Dinesen has pointed
out, at the heart of the story is a tale, something that can be
told, rather than an idea or mood.[11]

The storyteller's world is a world with firm outlines and
distinct texture on distance. The settings, the events, the
human beings that compose this world, are seen in perspective,
as if from a great height, complete and perfected.

The characters are types, never individuals, never "charac-
terless" (as Strindberg called the complex figures of his psychological dramas). They are larger than life, and their
behavior is artificial and stylized. The imagistic style of the
oral tale never delves deeply into their minds: abstract qualities and states of mind are rendered by means of concrete
images. The minds of men are things, as it were.[12] The names
of the figures and their gestures are exaggerated. They act
as if they were on the stage, plucking quotations out of the
air in order to define their roles, which are often re-enactments
of classical or mythical roles. The events are never unique
or isolated, but have already been fitted into an orderly pattern
in which they stand out very clearly within a meaningful
relationship: they have become ritual and myth.

The Past and the Far Away

The oral tradition of storytelling seems always to depend on a certain distance between the storyteller and his materials. The tapestry quality of a story by Dinesen is dependent on this perspective. As Staffan Björck has pointed out, this distance is Dinesen's "distinguishing mark as a writer, both means and end for the art of narrative she has chosen and the superiority of which she defends so unhesitatingly." It is, as Björck says, "only through the distance that the characters derive their definite outlines, the distance in descriptive technique, the distance in time and space, the distance in degree of reality to the unreal figures of the dream, the stage, and the marionette world." [13] A brief survey of the tales in regard to setting and character will indicate the accuracy of this observation.

With very few exceptions Dinesen's tales are set in the past. They are, however, not set in an indefinite past, but within a clearly defined period of time, the nineteenth century. Most of the tales bear clear indications of dates, and the greatest number of them are confined to the period between 1830 and 1875.

As far as the physical setting is concerned, Dinesen shows a decided preference for exotic milieus. Only in the *Winter's Tales* does the Danish setting seem to be predominant. France and southern Europe are the usual settings of the *Seven Gothic Tales*, and Italy is the scene of most of the *Last Tales*. Norway is the setting of several tales, and it must be remembered that in the early half of the nineteenth century Norway was still a wild and romantic country (AD, p. 71). Eight of the tales involve very exotic scenes: the West Indies, China, Persia, the Indian Ocean.

The reason for Dinesen's use of such exotic settings is

probably quite simple. The motive is undoubtedly similar to that of other writers of romance: a desire to liberate the imagination from the fetters which too familiar an environment imposes upon it.

When the English writers of Gothic tales, a Mrs. Radcliffe, a Horace Walpole, a "Monk" Lewis, chose the scenes for their tales, they usually selected an exotic setting in the past. Thus *The Mysteries of Udolpho* and *The Castle of Otranto* were set in Italy, and Lewis' *The Monk* in Spain.

"This longing for the south," says Eino Railo in his study of the Gothic writers in England, *The Haunted Castle,* "for any alien and distant setting, is typical of romanticism, and reflects the effort of their imagination to break away from the fetters of homely experience." To these Gothic writers the exotic setting was "a territory and an atmosphere where, freed from the narrow confines of their surroundings, their visions, passions and the characters with whom they dealt, could develop to dimensions that in any other connection would have been both impossible and unendurable." [14]

It comes as no surprise that Isak Dinesen, who must have used some of these writers of Gothic tales as models for her own romances, should employ a similar type of exotic setting in order to gain an equal degree of freedom to develop her fantastic plots.

The choice of the decades around 1830 and 1840 for many of the tales is probably not without significance. This is a time of social change: the values of *l'ancien régime* are in a state of rapid decline. It is the time of Louis Philippe, of the rise of the bourgeoisie to power, of Romanticism. For Dinesen with her definite aristocratic sympathies these decades must be of particular interest.

This is also a time which saw the publication of works by a great number of the writers with whom Isak Dinesen seems to have strong affinities. Some of the novels and tales of Hans Christian Andersen appeared during these decades, as did some of the most significant novels of Stendhal. Two French aristocrats, kindred spirits of Isak Dinesen, Barbey d'Aurevilly and Alfred de Vigny, published their best works during these years. Søren Kierkegaard, also a Gothic writer in many ways, published his novel *Either-Or* in 1843, and two other writers, Edgar Allan Poe and Eugène Sue, appeared on the scene, the former with a number of fantastic tales, the latter with *The Mysteries of Paris* in 1842-43 and *The Wandering Jew* in 1845, two Gothic masterpieces.

The reason for Dinesen's placing a number of the tales in the 1870's is somewhat more difficult to explain. These tales ("Copenhagen Season," "Babette's Feast," "The Old Chevalier") are usually less Gothic, more modern in spirit, and warmer in tone, if not nostalgic. They are frequently set in Paris. These tales also seem to render the actual life of the time more intimately, more concretely. One of the reasons for this is probably, as Christian Elling suggests, that these were years which Dinesen knew intimately through accounts by her father, who participated in the Franco-Prussian War and was in Paris during the uprising of the Commune (he also published a book about this event).[15]

While the 1870's seem to have been chosen by Dinesen in order to bring the figures in the tales somewhat closer to us, the intention in most of the tales is to remove the characters from us by placing them at a great distance in time and space. For this reason we find that the specific and detailed aspects of the setting are hardly ever rendered concretely or intimately, but in a fantastic, symbolic, or stylized manner.

The fantastic setting is, of course, most common in the purely Gothic tales. We need only think of Horace Walpole's

Strawberry Hill as a model. Convents, medieval castles in ruins, high mountains, deep forests, and the sea are common Gothic settings.

A good example of a fantastic setting in Dinesen's tales is Count Seraphina's Angelshorn in which Countess Calypso von Platen-Hallermund has been leading her unhappy life:

> The Count Seraphina had a great predilection for the Middle Ages. His huge castle of Angelshorn dated from that time, and he had taken pains to bring it back inside, as outside, to the times of the Crusades. It was not constructed, no more than was the Count himself, to spread itself much on earth, but the tall towers aspired to heaven, with a flight of jackdaws like a thin smoke around their heads, and the deep vaults seemed to dig themselves down toward the pit. The daylight was let in, between fathom-thick walls, through old stained glass, like cinnamon and blood of oxen, along the sides of the rooms, where, upon faded tapestries, unicorns were killed and the Magians and their retinue carried gold and myrrh to Bethlehem [SGT, p. 44].

Count Seraphina also imagined, in accordance with the Gothic fashion of the time, his castle to be "an abbey upon the northern soil," and himself "the abbot of a highly exclusive monastery" (SGT, p. 44).

In "The Monkey" we are introduced to Hopballehus, a fantastic two-hundred-year-old castle owned by Athena's father. To the young Boris von Schreckenstein it is a building "so enormous that it fell in with nature, and might have been a little formation of the gray rock," and he says that "it had always appealed to his imagination":

> It was in itself a fantastic place, resting upon a large plateau, with miles of avenues around it, rows of statues and fountains, built in late baroque and now baroquely dilapidated and more than half a ruin. It seemed a sort of Olympus, more Olympic still for the doom which was hanging over it [SGT, p. 122].

To Boris it is "a mysterious, a glorified, abode," and when he walks into it he has a feeling "like walking into a cathedral" (SGT, p. 123).

Deep in the forests of East Prussia is the convent Closter Seven, the setting of the main action in "The Monkey." The building does not seem fantastic: the strangeness of the convent is due to the fact that it is a kind of Noah's ark. It contains:

> . . . a whole world of pets of all sorts, and was well aware of the order of precedence therein. There were here parrots and cockatoos, small dogs, graceful cats from all parts of the world, a white Angora goat, like that of Esmeralda, and purple-eyed young fallow deer. There was even a tortoise which was supposed to be more than a hundred years old [SGT, p. 109].

In "The Caryatids" the water mill is a fantastic setting in which Childerique is introduced to magic and witchcraft by the gypsy. She thinks of the gypsy as a viper and of the mill as a viper's nest where strange and unknown powers are at work. In this story the setting mirrors Childerique's mood. We move from the idyllic forest glade with the mellow, golden light, and the green cool shade in the opening scenes, when Childerique is happy and ignorant of the curse, to the somber landscapes in the latter part of the story, with thunder and rain in the forest, when she has become acquainted with the truth about herself and her husband.

It is generally true of Dinesen's tales, as Brix maintains, that natural phenomena appear only when "they are intimately connected with the description of people." Nature and the landscape mirror terror, happiness, and sadness, reflecting various moods. The moon, winds, thunder and lightning, the night add a theatrical note which is undoubtedly intentional. The settings of most of the tales are meant to be artificial, props, backdrops for the stage on which the characters move like so many puppets.[16]

In "The Dreamers" Lincoln Forsner and his rivals pursue the fleeing Olalla (Pellegrina Leoni) by coach up into an Alpine pass where the climactic action takes place, ending with Olalla's death in a monastery. There are a wild moon, a driving snowstorm, howling winds, and drifting clouds. The terror of Olalla is reflected in the wildness of the elements, and the moon is the scenic light illuminating this opera extravaganza (SGT, pp. 317-28).

Thus Boris drives to Closter Seven in the moonlight with strong winds blowing about his carriage: "The moon was racing the heavens behind wild thin clouds; the air was cold. . . . His lanterns chased the trees and their shadows and threw them to all sides around him." He is gripped by terror, feeling that strange powers are afoot: "The feeling was so strong and distinct that it was as if an ice-cold hand had passed for a moment over his scalp. His hair rose a little upon his head. For a few minutes he was really and genuinely afraid, struck by an extraordinary terror" (SGT, pp. 132-33).

In some of the tales the setting is, however, purely symbolic. This is the case in "Sorrow Acre." Here the landscape and the buildings form a geometric figure, a pyramid, which becomes a symbolic representation of the feudal organization of life. The irregular mosaic of meadows and cornfields tells of the life of the peasants, as does "the blurred outline of thatched roofs." A little higher up lies the red-tiled church "with the faint horizontal line of white cemetery-wall" around it. The church is described as a "plain, square embodiment of the nation's trust in the justice and mercy of heaven." "But where, amongst cupular woods and groves, the lordly, pyramidal silhouette of the cut lime avenues rose in the air, there a big country house lay." The lime trees parade around the manor and form a "green pyramid," speaking of "dignity, decorum, and taste." In this setting, plainly symbolic, a story of human suffering and human dignity is unfolded, illustrating the order on which this feudal world is based (WT, pp. 29-30).

In "The Pearl" the bourgeois Jensine panics at the sight of the Norwegian mountains, having believed that nature was and should be horizontal in expansion as in the low, undulating Danish landscape. In Norway she is introduced to a new dimension of life, while her husband, who knows neither fear nor terror, is at home in the vertical realm: the mountains are his playground. In this story about courage and fear the mountains are a symbolic, moral landscape (WT, p. 109).

One of the basic features of Dinesen's art is her tendency to transform all of life into artifice. Very often she looks at the landscape with a painter's eye, and it is significant to note that the author once intended to become a painter. Christian Elling comments also on the fact that Dinesen seems to use paintings as models for her descriptions of nature. He quotes her as admitting: "I have always had difficulty in seeing how a landscape really looked, unless I had received the key to it from a great painter. . . . Constable, Gainsborough and Turner have shown me England." [17]

In some cases descriptions are rendered through the use of metaphors and similes: the landscape is compared to a work of art. In "Sorrow Acre" it is said that "the fields, the hills, and the woods were as still as a painted landscape" (WT, p. 47). In "The Poet" a similar type of description is used: "The rich hues of night have withdrawn, oozed away like the waves from a shore, and all the colors of daytime lie dormant in the landscape like in the paints used for pottery, which are all alike gray clay until they come out in the furnace" (SGT, p. 374).

33

Heroes and Heroines

The world of Isak Dinesen contains a large gallery of characters. Sometimes one character appears in several tales, but that is an exception to the rule: Augustus von Schimmelmann appears both in "The Roads Round Pisa" and in "The Poet," and the storyteller Mira Jama both in "The Dreamers" and in "The Diver."

Most of the characters are colorful and vivid figures with splendid names, original ideas, and exciting lives. Many are aristocrats, high-ranking people of noble birth—kings, princes, and cardinals. About half of them are artists or somehow involved with the arts. Many are students of theology, highly interested in religious speculations. With regard to their character traits, they fall into a few fairly well-defined categories, or types.

THE MELANCHOLIACS

The first type is the standard hero or heroine of much Romantic literature: the melancholy young man or woman, so fashionable in the literature of the 1830's and 1840's. We need only think of Kierkegaard's Frater Taciturnus or Stendhal's Lucien Leuwen. This Hamlet figure, very common in Danish literature, appears in various guises in the tales. He is the observer of life, contemplating himself thoughtfully in the mirror, wondering about the truth and the meaning of existence, unable to commit himself to any course of action, waiting for fate to lend him a helping hand.

Thus Count Augustus von Schimmelmann sits in an *osteria* near Pisa waiting for fate to give him a sign (SGT, p. 167). He is said to be "of melancholy disposition," and he contemplates himself thoughtfully in a little pocket mirror on

34

several occasions (SGT, pp. 165-66, 216). He thinks about truth. Some years later he reappears in "The Poet," older, but still of the same "heavy and melancholy disposition": "He wanted to be happy but he had no talent for happiness" (SGT, p. 380). He is a dilettante, a fine connoisseur of art and pleasure.

Prince Giovanni in "The Roads Round Pisa" is possessed of a melancholy "about which the whole province grieves" (SGT, p. 189).

The two De Coninck sisters in "The Supper at Elsinore," Fanny and Eliza, are "born melancholiacs" who talk of life "with the black bitterness of two Timons of Athens," and feel unreal in their relation to the world as if they were only two reflections in a mirror (SGT, pp. 219-20). "The fatal melancholy of the family" has also affected the young hero of "true romance," their brother Morten, the hero of Elsinore (SGT, p. 221).

Axel Leth in "The Invincible Slaveowners" is a young Dane who suffers from melancholy thoughts and contemplates the stars, suffering from "the sham of his world" (WT, pp. 132, 135). He resembles another young Dane, Jonathan Maersk in "The Deluge at Norderney," another Timon of Athens (or "Assens" as the story has it). Disgusted by the deceit and sham of the world of fashion, he has become a melancholy figure who comtemplates suicide. Ironically enough his melancholy has made him more fashionable still, melancholy being then (the 1830's) a cloak of fashion made popular by Lord Byron, Alfred de Musset, Chopin, and Chateaubriand (SGT, pp. 28-40).

The writer Charlie Despard (whose very name suggests despair), the hero of two of the *Winter's Tales,* is a young melancholiac, "sunk in gloom" and sick to death (WT, p. 3). He is said to be "subject to that particular sadness which is expressed in the old saying: *omne animal post coitum triste,*" and suffers from "a strong sense of the emptiness and vanity of all human ambitions" (WT, pp. 289-90).

King Erik Glipping of Denmark in "The Fish," a melancholy figure who identifies himself with Ahasverus and feels as lonely as God, is weary of responsibility, envy, and ambition; he feels that all is vanity, and longs for a fuller task and things that are unattainable (WT, pp. 228-35).

THE IRRESISTIBLE ONES

A second rather common type in Dinesen's gallery is the stereotyped fearless hero or heroine of romance who embraces life and danger with courage and pride. These characters, whom Elling refers to as "the irresistible ones," are usually found among the aristocrats.[18] They are very different from the members of the bourgeoisie, who are imbued with fear, afraid to commit themselves, and unwilling to pay the price of life.

Morten De Coninck is a melancholy figure like his two sisters, but he is also one of the irresistible ones, a heroic figure without knowledge of fear or guilt who has had the courage to say no to the secure and comfortable life in Elsinore which has stifled the spirits of Fanny and Eliza. His great love and passion are his ship and the sea.

Heloise in "The Heroine" not only bears a name that reminds someone of "all the sound of heroic French history," but she is like a lioness, and not the least afraid, in spite of the precarious situation in which she finds herself (WT, p. 73). Confronted with the danger of the moment "she became," says Frederick, "still more heraldic, like a lioness in a coat of arms" (WT, p. 74). She is a master of the world "and will stand no nonsense from it. She is the descendant and the rightful heiress, of conquerors and commanders, even of tyrants, of this world" (WT, p. 75).

In "The Pearls" Alexander is a dashing Romantic hero who prefers the vertical Norway to the placid and horizontal Denmark because he is, unlike his wife Jensine, devoid of fear (WT, p. 110). Unlike Jensine he does not worry about tomorrow. In the same story Henrik Ibsen appears in the guise of the artist as hero: he is not afraid to commit himself to a career as a dramatist, though it is a path full of uncertainties and difficulties.

THE POSSESSED

A third major group of characters is composed of those whom we might call the possessed, the fanatics, characters whose lives are governed by an idea.

Miss Malin Nat-og-Dag is possessed by an idea. Being "a lady of the strictest virtue," she has for years believed herself "to be one of the great female sinners of her time" (SGT, p. 9). She is accompanied by Countess Calypso von Platen-Hallermund and together they give an appearance of "wildness." They are likened to two tigresses, "the cub quite wild, the old one only the more dangerous for having the appearance of being tamed." Neither of them is the least bit afraid in the situation in which they find themselves. Miss Malin is totally indifferent to fate, and Calypso is possessed by "that simple and arrogant optimism which takes for granted that nothing can go wrong" (SGT, p. 10). Both of them are proud and fanatic aristocrats.

Lady Flora Gordon in "The Cardinal's Third Tale" is also, like Miss Nat-og-Dag, "a fanatic virgin" (SGT, p. 18). She is also a proud aristocrat whose loathing of humanity is of such magnitude that it is compared to Jonathan Swift's. She is suspicious of all of creation and of the Creator. She is supremely arrogant, shrinks from any touch, and lives in proud and splendid isolation.

The prioress in "The Monkey" is undoubtedly one of the possessed, though in her case it is not by an idea but by a little demon, a gray monkey (which might, of course, be said to represent the idea of freedom). In the fall, in particular, the monkey usually feels "the call of a freer life and would disappear for a few weeks or a month." At such times, according to the opinion of the ladies of the convent, the prioress "would become silent and the victim of a particular restlessness, and would seem loth to act in the affairs of the house, in which at ordinary times she showed great vigor" (SGT, p. 110).

In the same tale Athena of Hopballehus is not only a giantess, she is also a fanatic Republican. She has "a pair of eyes for a young lioness or eagle," and the peculiar habit of standing "on one leg, like a big stork" (SGT, pp. 129-30). She is a great admirer of Danton, and would, if she could, "cut off the heads of all the tyrants of Europe" (SGT, p. 132). Like Flora Gordon she is a Diana, "a fanatical virgin" (SGT, p. 137).

In Dinesen's tales the women predominate among the possessed. The old Lady Carlotta in "The Roads Round Pisa" is possessed by the idea that all women in her family will die in childbirth and involves herself in all sorts of intrigues in order to prevent them from becoming with child. The two sisters in "The Invincible Slaveowners" are so fanatically attached to their family pride they take turns at disguising themselves as each other's servant at Baden-Baden. Babette, once a fanatic *pétroleuse* in the Paris of the Commune, is so devoted to her art of cooking that she spends a fortune preparing one meal.

There are, however, a few men among the possessed. Kasparson, royal bastard, valet, and actor, wants to play a great role once in his life, and is willing to go to any lengths in order to realize his ambition. Johannes Ewald in "Converse at Night" is possessed by the idea of "mythos." The hero of "A Country Tale," Squire Eitel, is possessed by the idea of justice, and feels that he must atone for the injustice done to the peasants by his father. The young Saufe in "The Diver" is possessed by the idea of being able to fly like the birds because birds "must be, of all creatures, most like angels" (AD, p. 3).

By placing the action of the tales in the past and in far away lands, Dinesen frees her imagination from the restrictions that too familiar an environment would impose upon it. And by creating a great distance between the storyteller and the characters of his story, she transforms the figures in the tales, she succeeds in transforming them into "luminous" heroes and heroines who appear larger than life and on a "higher plane."

A World of Likenesses

One of the outstanding features of Dinesen's style is, as has already been noted, her use of metaphors and similes. Like Father Jacopo in "The Cardinal's Third Tale" she seems to feel "that it is wise and pious to call attention to likenesses" (LT, p. 85). It is important to consider here not only what types of metaphors and similes are used but what in particular inspires the author to use them. Many of these figures of speech fall into one of three categories: those involving animals, those involving flowers, and those involving marionettes (see pp. 15-19). All of them serve for the most part to exaggerate the proportions of the characters and to remove them from the ordinary human plane.

In connection with a discussion specifically of Dinesen's

use of metaphors and similes involving animals, it is interesting to note her fondness for animal imagery in general. Bird images are the most common, with the swan recurring more frequently than any other particular bird. Among the numerous wild animals the lioness, tigress, and lion cub are notably common. And there are many images of snakes and fish.

One might speculate on the reasons for Dinesen's great fondness for animal imagery. Her twenty years among the many exotic animals of Africa must have influenced her greatly in this respect. Incidentally, in Africa Dinesen was herself referred to as a "lioness" by the natives. Her reading of LaFontaine and Aesop, and of the Bible, must have had a great influence on her style. Finally, there is the possible influence of her father, who was a great lover of animals.

Some examples of Dinesen's use of animal metaphors and similes will indicate the functions which they serve.

Miss Nat-og-Dag is one of the most colorful figures in the tales. Along with Calypso she is imbued with the racial pride of a vanishing aristocracy, and has an appearance of wildness: "To the rescuing party it was as if they had taken into the boat two tigresses, one old and one young, the cub quite wild, the old one only the more dangerous for having the appearance of being tamed" (SGT, p. 9). Being a "fanatical virgin" she has always been on the lookout "like a fighting-bull for a red cloth, or a crusader for the sign of the half-moon, for any sign of the eye of lust, in order to annihilate the owner without pity" (SGT, p. 18). When at the age of twenty-seven she finally decided to choose one of her suitors, "she felt like a very tall bitch surrounded by small yapping lap dogs" (SGT, p. 19). Having come into a great fortune at the age of fifty, she has been liberated from most earthly cares. When that happened, "a weight fell away from her; she flew up to a higher perch and cackled a little" (SGT, p. 20).

Through the use of similar figures of speech involving animals Athena von Hopballchus becomes a grotesque figure. She is said to have "a pair of eyes for a young lioness or eagle," and she stands on one leg "like a big stork" (SGT, pp. 129-30). During the seduction scene in which Boris thinks of himself as a bull in the Madrid arena, Athena draws herself up "as a snake does when it is ready to strike" (SGT, p. 152). She is compared to "a young she bear," relying on her great strength, and she has a "lioness's roar deep within her voice" (SGT, pp. 154, 159).

While these animal images serve to make the figures in the tales into grotesque, sometimes comic, larger than life characters, the similes and metaphors pertaining to flowers serve to remove the characters from the realm of individuality to the realm of symbol.

Flowers are invariably used in connection with women. The most common is the image of the rose.

When Baron von Brackel first meets Nathalie in "The Old Chevalier," he wonders at her, "as one would wonder at finding a fresh bunch of roses in a gutter" (SGT, p. 91). Her undressing inspires him to speak of the woman of "those days," those days when woman was like a perfect work of art. He speaks of the waist shooting up "like the chalice of a flower, carrying the bust, high and rounded as a rose." In those days clothes were designed to disguise, not to reveal, the body: for this reason it was indeed "a revelation to us every time she stepped out of her disguise, with her waist still delicately marked by the stays, as with a girdle of rose petals." In those days there was no question as to which was more important, the idea of woman, or the individual woman. Women were brought up to become representatives of the idea of woman: "slowly the center of gravity of her being would be shifted from individuality to symbol" (SGT, p. 94).

Isak Dinesen has often indicated that in her attitude concerning women she is a kindred spirit to Baron von Brackel. In a talk given in 1953 she expressed some of her now undoubtedly old-fashioned views about men and women and the differences between them.[19] To Dinesen man is the being who acts: "A man's center of gravity, the quality of his being, consists of what he accomplishes and does in life." The woman, on the other hand, has her center of gravity in "what she is" (p. 18). A man *does* something, a woman *is* something (beautiful, charming) or *means* something by her very being (like the Virgin Mary or the Maid of Orleans) (p. 20). Men think in terms of the result of an action or activity, women find their fulfillment in the activity itself (embroidery). As artists men create works of art while women become, or are, works of art (actresses, singers, dancers) (pp. 22-23). The power of woman is the power of the acorn, which is powerful by virtue of its fidelity toward its own nature (pp. 33-34).

With this distinction between men and women and its emphasis on the idea of woman rather than the individual, it is not surprising that the flower—the rose in particular—is employed in the tales as a symbol of the idea of woman. Like the acorn, the flower is what it is; and it is powerful insofar as it fulfills its own nature.

This correspondence between the idea of woman and the rose is developed in "A Country Tale." A young woman and a young man are walking in the wood. No word is spoken. The young woman lets her glance glide lovingly and happily over the forest scenery, while the young man ponders the vocation of man. To the young man it is as if he did not himself see the landscape before him, "but only through her knew that it existed, and what it meant." Then the similarity between the young woman's being and the rose is developed:

42

She did not turn toward him; she rarely did so, and very rarely on her own offered a caress. Her form and color, the fall of her rich dark hair and the lines of her shoulders, her long hands and slim knees, in themselves were caresses; her entire being and nature was to enchant, and she craved for nothing else in life.

The young man thinks: "The vocation of a rose is to exhale scent; for that reason do we plant roses in our garden. But a rose on its own exhales a sweeter scent than we could ever demand of it. It craves for nothing else in life" (LT, pp. 192-93). The young man, however, returns to his thoughts.

In "The Roads Round Pisa" both Agnese and Rosina are compared to oleander flowers (SGT, pp. 206, 214). In "The Heroine" Heloise is compared to a rose (WT, p. 73), and Mizzi in "The Invincible Slaveowners" is seen as "a high-stemmed rose" (WT, p. 129), and has "a flaming mouth, like a red rose": "Looking at it one might well imagine the whole straight, proud figure to exist only in order to carry this fresh, presumptuous mouth about the world" (WT, p. 130). The people about her are seen as so many "bees and butterflies . . . humming round the new fair, fragrant rose" (WT, p. 133). Later she is praised "as a great lady in the bud, a maiden brought up on the high principles of the old world, and undefiled by any low contact, a rose, a young swan" (WT, p. 150).

In "Copenhagen Season" Adelaide von Galen is called "The Rose of Jutland,"

. . . as if all the land of the peninsula, from the dunes of the Skague to the pastures of Friesland, had gone to make up soil for this one fragrant, fragile flower. The rose swayed pliantly to the breezes, youthfully and naively alluring in color and scent, but it stood on an exceedingly high hill [LT, p. 256].

Here the rose metaphor seems to suggest the idea of woman as a prize, a value, only to be obtained through some kind of

43

heroic action. It is significant that the image of the rose is most frequently used in those tales which center around one of Dinesen's central motifs, the motif of aristocratic pride and heroism.

Literary and Mythical Roles

There is a second device by which Dinesen removes her characters from the ordinary human plane and places them on a larger-than-human footing. That is the device of using literary and mythical references metaphorically, i.e., of comparing the characters to familiar figures from literature and mythology.

Thus Kasparson in "The Deluge at Norderney" is called "a curious Sancho Panza for the noble knight of the church" (SGT, p. 5). Miss Nat-og-Dag is compared to Sigrid the Haughty, ancient Queen of Norway, who once "summoned to her all her suitors amongst the minor kings of the country, and then put fire to the house and burned them all up, declaring that in this way she would teach the petty kings of Norway to come and woo her" (SGT, pp. 17-18). Jonathan Maersk plays the role of the melancholy Timon of Athens (SGT, pp. 28-40). Calypso, when she went to cut off her breasts, "took a candlestick in one hand and a sharp hatchet in the other, like to Judith when she went to kill Holophernes" (SGT, p. 46).

Nathalie in "The Old Chevalier" appears miraculously out of nowhere "like Cinderella, or a little spirit out of the Arabian Nights" (SGT, p. 102).

In "The Monkey" the old Count appears at the top step, "standing like Samson when in his wrath he broke down the temple of the Philistines" (SGT, p. 124). As he comes down the steps, his presence is "such as the Lord himself might have shown had he descended, for once, the ladder of Jacob" (SGT, p. 124). Athena makes Boris think of the "old ballad about the giant's daughter, who finds a man in the wood, and, surprised and pleased, takes him home to play with" (SGT, p. 129). Later she is called a "Diana" (SGT, p. 137). Boris becomes "one of the Einherjar of Valhalla" as he struggles with Athena (SGT, p. 153).

Rosina in "The Roads Round Pisa" is "as lovely as the young St. Michele himself commanding the heavenly hosts" (SGT, p. 173). Prince Nino looks like "any young St. Sebastian or John the Baptist, living on wild honey and locust, or even a young angel from the opened sepulcher" (SGT, p. 186). Prince Pozentiani has "the soft fullness, and the great power behind it, of the ancient statues of Bacchus" (SGT, p. 193). Prince Nino describes Agnese as "my picture of Daphne, who turns away and is changed into a laurel" (SGT, p. 209).

In "The Cardinal's Third Tale" Flora Gordon is like a giantess from *Gulliver's Travels,* and her friends liken her to Diana (LT, p. 95).

Herr Soerensen, the old theater director in "Tempests," is compared to Prospero, whose role in Shakespeare's play he is enacting in the story; and Malli Ross, his young protégée, is Ariel (AD, p. 88).

In "The Immortal Story" Virginie says to Elishama, Mr. Clay's clerk: "When you came in, I thought that you were a small rat, out of Mr. Clay's storehouses. *Mais toi—tu es le Juif Errant!"* (AD, p. 194).

In Dinesen's world the names of the characters are often very significant. Some of them are, of course, rather ordinary names (Anders Kube, Jens Jespersen), but others are so exaggerated that they become grotesque or humorous. Unlike most contemporary writers, who give to their figures rather common, everyday names (or no names at all), Dinesen is fond of long picturesque names such as Calypso von Platen-Hallermund, Boris von Schreckenstein, Hamilcar von Sehestedt, Augustus von Schimmelmann, or Adelaide von Galen.

In some cases the names are significant in that they point toward some mythical or literary role being enacted by the character. In "Sorrow Acre" Adam is probably enacting such a mythical role.

At other times the derivation of the name is indicative of the role played by the figure. As Elling points out, the name Kasparson suggests a derivation from the name Caspar Hauser, the famous adventurer, and Kasperle, the marionette figure.[20] Olalla resembles the character by the same name in a short story by Robert Louis Stevenson entitled "Olalla."[21] Boris von Schreckenstein has a name not surprisingly composed of the German word for terror, and "-stein," probably from the famous Gothic figure Frankenstein.

Theatricality

The third method used by Dinesen to make her figures larger than life is the exaggeration of physical appearances, gestures, and physiological effects. It is safe to say, I think, that the figures in contemporary fiction are largely of average physical appearance. What they look like does not matter very much. In *Barabbas* Pär Lagerkvist wastes little space describing the hero because "a man's appearance is of little consequence."[22] With this lack of emphasis on physical appearance goes the avoidance of the theatrical effects of exaggerated gestures and physiological reactions. In Dinesen's world the contrary is true. Many of the figures in the tales are remembered because of their unusual physical qualities. The expressive gesture is very common, and physiological changes are used on the whole to indicate emotional changes. Dinesen's figures undergo great changes of appearance under the influence of passion. This is, of course, a very characteristic feature of the art of romance.

Dinesen's emphasis on physical traits that are out of the ordinary can be seen clearly in her description of the two giantesses, Athena and Flora Gordon. Miss Nat-og-Dag has a very large nose, and it is often mentioned (SGT, pp. 17, 19). In some cases such descriptions are used for a purely comic effect. Thus in "Copenhagen Season" the painter's face is said to look like the posterior of an infant (LT, p. 269).

Exaggerated gestures and physiological reactions are frequent particularly in the *Seven Gothic Tales*. In "The Deluge at Norderney" the four people just rescued sit in the boat "white as corpses" (SGT, p. 9). Jonathan turns pale at the sight of the collapsing granary (SGT, p. 11). The Cardinal falls down "in a dead faint" (SGT, p. 16), and when he wakes up he "stares wildly at them." Miss Nat-og-Dag blushes (SGT, p. 24), and when Jonathan is to tell his story the color rises in his pale cheeks (SGT, p. 28). At the sound of the name August von Platen-Hallermund, Calypso shudders and grows pale, and a "threatening dusk" sinks over her clear eyes (SGT, p. 42). She turns her eyes on Jonathan with "such an intense and frantic look as if life and death for her depended upon his answer" (SGT, p. 51). When she hears it her face suddenly pales into "a rare pearly white," and her eyes seem to Jonathan to grow "bigger and darker. They shone at him like stars with a moisture deeper than tears, and at the sight of her changed face Jonathan sank upon his knees before her in the hay" (SGT, pp. 51-52). Miss Malin looks "like a corpse of twenty-four hours," and after the marriage ceremony "long

shudders ran through her from head to feet" (SGT, p. 55).
She turns pale, "her mouth a little open," as Kasparson talks
about the fall in heaven (SGT, p. 56). Calypso again turns
deadly pale and sinks down in the hay (SGT, p. 70). When
she hears the truth from Kasparson, the old woman's lips turn
"white and stiff," and Kasparson is "a pale man" (SGT, p.
74). In the final scene Miss Malin's eyes are "radiant" as she
names Kasparson "Bastard of Egalité" and orders him to kiss
her (SGT, p. 78).

These physiological effects and exaggerated gestures are so
common that the number of examples could be multiplied
greatly. "The Dreamers" affords innumerable examples.

In *Winter's Tales* the element of exaggeration is toned
down somewhat, but the note of theatricality is still very evident. In "Sorrow Acre," for example, Dinesen uses exaggerated gestures in order to achieve a stylized and elevated
effect.

The old uncle has a "grand, ceremonial manner" about him
even when he solemnly proclaims that "it will be a hot day"
(WT, p. 37). He speaks with "his majestic nose a little in the
air" (WT, p. 38), and "gravely" or with "deep gravity" (WT,
p. 39). For his wife he is "a stately consort" (WT, p. 46).
Speaking to Adam about the divine art of comedy he appears
as an "erect, ceremonious prophet" (WT, p. 52). Perplexed
by Adam's outbursts he turns around with an expression in
his eyes of "stately surprise" (WT, p. 56). His long, waxen
face "with two symmetrical curls at the sides" has for Adam
"something of the mien of an idealized and ennobled old
sheep or ram," and he speaks "with hauteur" (WT, p. 56).
Adam, on the other hand, "cries out" in "despair" and exclaims
at the injustice of the old lord (WT, p. 57). The gestures of
the uncle are stiff (WT, p. 62). As the tragedy of Anne-
Marie nears its appointed end he dresses up "in a brocaded

suit that he had worn at Court." The movements of Anne-Marie as she cuts the corn appear more and more like the movements in a divine rite (WT, p. 64).

The actions and gestures of the old lord in "Sorrow Acre" illustrate how a strong emphasis on expressive gesture produces a theatrical effect. The theater is an important element in Dinesen's world. Her figures are actors and actresses in plots that are like theatrical extravaganzas. They are often imbued with a strong sense of the fact that they are, in effect, acting in a tragedy, or a comedy, or a ballet, or a ritual of some sort.

The old uncle in "Sorrow Acre" is acting a part in a kind of ritual, but also in a tragedy (Anne-Marie's) and in a comedy (his own). There are many instances in the tales of such theatrical and mythical performances.

Kasparson in "The Deluge at Norderney" is by profession an actor and plays his role as the Cardinal to the hilt. From the very first moment he behaves like an actor. When the people of the resort applaud his heroism he bows "his head a little, with an exquisite irony, in the manner of a hero upon the stage" (SGT, p. 9). The final scene between Kasparson and Miss Nat-og-Dag is grand theater (SGT, pp. 77-79). The hayloft becomes a *salon* under Miss Nat-og-Dag's tutelage (SGT, pp. 15-16), and the marriage ceremony is pure theater (SGT, pp. 52-54).

In "The Monkey" Boris is acting: "The deepest and truest thing" in his nature is "his great love for the stage and all its ways" (SGT, p. 140). To Boris the theater is real life. On the evening of the seduction he feels his friends would have been delighted with him for "he had never played better." With great care he applies his mask before the mirror and decides to wear black in order to accentuate the role of the unhappy lover. Looking at Athena, he is pleased "with his *jeune première* of the night. Now that they were upon the stage together he read her like a book" (SGT, p. 141).

In "The Roads Round Pisa" all of the figures are playing in a marionette comedy and are, as such, not really aware of the fact that they are actors in a play. The scene between Agnese and Prince Nino is, however, highly conscious theater (SGT, pp. 208-10). Speaking to each other of their strange adventure, they quote lines from Dante's *Divina Commedia*.

In "The Dreamers" Pellegrina Leoni is an actress, and it is, as a result, not surprising that she plays a part in what appears to Lincoln Forsner as a "theatrical extravaganza." She masquerades herself as Rosalba, as Olalla, as Madame Lola, always playing a part. Ultimately, we learn she is also playing a part in a ballet composed by Marcus Cocoza, a ballet about her adventures and impersonations.

In several of the *Winter's Tales* the figures are really playing appointed parts in a myth or ritual, but as with the marionette figures in "The Roads Round Pisa" they are not aware of their roles. For this reason their behavior cannot be termed consciously theatrical. Jens in "The Dreaming Child," Alkmene, and the sailor boy play such roles.

In the *Last Tales* there are two examples of pure theater. In "Copenhagen Season" Ib and his sister play in a classical tragedy, and in "Converse at Night" Johannes Ewald and the King act in a kind of opera buffa or ballet, Johannes Ewald as Yorick and the King as Orosman.

In "Tempests" the conversation between Herr Soerensen and Malli Ross models itself after the lines of Shakespeare's play.

An additional feature might be mentioned. This is the habit of some of the figures in the tales to pluck quotations out of the air and use them very consciously. A good example is seen in the final speech of the fish in "The Diver": "Man, in the end, is alarmed by the idea of time, and unbalanced by incessant wanderings between past and future. The inhabitants of the liquid world have brought past and future together in the maxim: *Après nous le déluge"* (AD, p. 20).

Comedy and Humor

In a recent interview Isak Dinesen spoke of the comic spirit in her stories: "I do often intend a comic sense, I love a joke, I love the humorous. I often think that what we most need now is a great humorist." Asked what humorists she likes to read, she answered that "all the writers I admire usually have a vein of comic spirit. Writers of tales always do, at least." [23]

The last remark is an interesting observation. The storyteller tends, as we have seen, to regard life from a distance, and so does the comic artist. As things seem to hurt less when they have been put into a story, so life takes on the quality of being a great human comedy when regarded from a distance. To tell tales is to be a humorist. If the story is a divine art, so is comedy.

The world of Dinesen is permeated with a comic vision of life. It is perhaps best defined as a kind of romantic irony, often found among some of the storytellers Dinesen admires: E. T. A. Hoffmann, for instance. In the final analysis, it is a profound humor.

Dinesen the romantic ironist is the Baroness Blixen hiding behind a number of pseudonyms. Like many modern writers Karen Blixen places herself at an ironic distance from her own stories. Osceola, Pierre Andrézel, Isak Dinesen: these are three pseudonyms, and the tales published under these names are, in addition, frequently told by narrators who do, or do not, participate in the action. This is, of course, a common technique among contemporary writers, who are fond of ambiguity and complexity. It is an element of Dinesen's art which must be kept in mind when we try to define the nature of the imagination that has projected the world of the tales. Isak Dinesen, like her famous countryman Søren Kierkegaard, alias Victor Eremita, is an artist of the mask and a master of irony.

A further aspect of Dinesen's romantic irony has to do with her attitude to art and the artist, to the story and the storyteller. We have already spoken of Dinesen's loyalty to the story, of her defense of the story. In the universe of story which she creates, God Himself is a great storyteller, but also a great charlatan, God and Devil in the same person. Thus the storyteller, God's representative here on earth, is also a bit of a charlatan. There is in Dinesen's tales an attitude toward the artist which is similar to Thomas Mann's: the artist is not quite respectable, he is a confidence man; it is by no means certain whether he is in the service of God or the Devil. The storyteller is seen in an ironic light. Even the story, no matter how divine, is a form of deception, an illusion, a dream, disguising the essential nothingness of life. As such it does, however, become a heroic defiance of nothingness, for it requires courage to meet the deception of life with a still greater form of deception.

The tales are, of course, filled with various comic effects, and life as a whole is often conceived as a human comedy authored by a comic divinity who "loves a joke." But Dinesen's comic vision goes deeper than that, and it is for this reason that I choose to call it humor.

Humor blends laughter and tears, joy and sorrow, pleasure and pain. There is in Dinesen's tales, says Jørgen Gustava Brandt, a feeling of "life as play, game, and as tragic seriousness." [24] Comedy and tragedy are interwoven. Like Adam in

"Sorrow Acre" Dinesen seems to feel that one must come to terms with contradiction, suffering, and pain before life can really begin. This is a conception of humor very close to that expressed by some of the German Romantics. In humor the German Romantics discovered, says William G. O'Donnell in a recent essay on Kierkegaard's humor, "a deep, enduring, warmhearted, Germanic feeling of kinship with all forms of life. It rests upon a sympathy for one's fellow-sufferers in a world out of joint. It springs from the heart and is almost another name for love." [25] This kind of humor is very common in many of the tales: the insight into life which so many of Dinesen's heroes and heroines receive is very often precisely of this nature.

Humor, as understood by Isak Dinesen, is an affirmation and acceptance of life in all its forms, the opposite of rebellion. Writing from Germany during the last war, from a society dedicated to the belief in the omnipotence of the human will, Dinesen spoke of her own faith in the one attitude to life which was forbidden in Germany: "The strange kind of reliance on the grace of God, which one calls humor." [26]

Humor is then a kind of yes-saying to life, an acceptance of whatever fate will bring, and the theme of acceptance is a profound one in Dinesen's tales. But, in saying yes to life, the figures in the tales are also acknowledging the authority of the story and the divine storyteller. Thus Dinesen weaves her tales in such a way that the two themes become one: acceptance of life is a defense of the story. It is no surprise, for this reason, that Dinesen is fond of telling the old tales all over again, that she is a writer of pastiche, for old stories become myths, patterns that God has found useful over and over again.

2
THE
GOTHIC
TALE

THE ART of Isak Dinesen has often been called an art of pastiche. When *Seven Gothic Tales* appeared in Denmark, the late poet and critic Paul la Cour spoke of the disappointment he experienced when reading Dinesen's stories. La Cour maintained that they were mere pastiche and lacking in feeling, because they were not motivated by an inner vision demanding expression. They were merely told for the sake of telling a good story.[1]

The late Harald Nielsen, a severe critic of Dinesen's works, concentrated his criticism on her dependence on the decadent tradition in European literature, finding in the tales a "lack of living humanity" which he attributed to the author's habit of dwelling too frequently on the sadistic fantasies of diabolical old men or the perverse manipulations of wicked old women.[2]

Many of Dinesen's tales are undoubtedly both Gothic and decadent. The spine-chilling tale of terror, with its persecuted women, its ghosts, and its mysterious convents and castles, as well as the cruel tale, with its atmosphere of perversity and artificiality, have served as sources of inspiration for Dinesen. The tales of Horace Walpole, E. T. A. Hoffmann, and Barbey d'Aurevilly come to mind.

Yet, one hesitates to call Dinesen's tales mere pastiche. Dinesen's dependence on the Gothic and decadent tradition is evident, but the significant fact concerning this dependence is the manner in which she makes this tradition serve her own vision.

All but two of the tales in Dinesen's first collection are Gothic tales. All of them are Gothic and decadent tales, there being, in my opinion, no significant difference between the qualities which we term Gothic and those which we term decadent.[3] The *Winter's Tales* and the *Last Tales* are very seldom Gothic tales, the one notable exception being "The Caryatids," subtitled "An Unfinished Gothic Tale," which was originally to have been included in *Seven Gothic Tales*. "The Immortal Story" in *Anecdotes of Destiny* is a decadent tale. The novel, *The Angelic Avengers*, is a piece of entertainment in the genre of the Gothic novel.

"The Monkey" is Dinesen's finest Gothic tale. It has the perfect Gothic setting; it creates an atmosphere of mystery and terror; it has a decadent hero; and it develops several typical Gothic motifs: the double, innocence pursued, sadism, and exoticism.

The setting has already been described. Athena's home, Hopballehus, is also referred to as "a fantastic place" which had always "appealed to his [Boris'] imagination" as "a mysterious abode" in which nothing stirs, and which lies there "majestic as the Sphinx herself in the sunset" (SGT, p. 123).

The main action is set in a convent, a favorite haunt of

Gothic writers. Around the convent strange and mysterious powers are afoot. As Boris drives to the convent he feels that "strange powers were out tonight" (SGT, p. 133). His hair rises on his head, and he is "struck by an extraordinary terror," feeling himself "absurdly small, exposed and unsafe." As his britzska turns a corner, the lamps shine into a pair of glinting eyes. In "the disquieting night" the moon, that old stage light of romance, is "racing the heavens behind wild thin clouds," and the wind is "singing." As Boris walks to Athena's room through the typical long corridor, the moon stands high in the heavens, "clear and cold" (SGT, p. 150).

Other elements of mystery and horror are provided through the transformation of the aunt into a monkey. On the morning after the seduction, Boris, Athena, and the aunt are speaking together when all of a sudden there is a sharp knocking on one of the windowpanes. This knocking has an extraordinary effect on the aunt: "she was immediately struck by a deadly terror." She grows "white as a corpse," her arms and legs move "in little jerks," and her eyes dart "up and down the walls." Seeing the monkey outside the window, Boris wants to let it in, but the aunt shrieks "No! No!" in "a paroxysm of horror." During the struggle with the monkey the old woman shivers "in a horrible passion," grinds her teeth, acts as "if blinded by fright," and her face is "transformed, shriveled and wrinkled, and of dark-brown color" (SGT, pp. 160-61).

The central motif of the tale is that of the double, common in Gothic literature. We need only think of Menardus in *Die Elixire des Teufels,* or Ambrosio in Lewis' *The Monk,* or Stevenson's *Dr. Jekyll and Mr. Hyde,* or the jeweler in Hoffmann's *Mademoiselle de Scudéry.*

The prioress evidently possesses a double nature. In the fall, it is said, the monkey often feels the need for a freer life, and is apt to disappear into the forest for a few weeks. At such times the prioress is also said to be the victim of a particular restlessness (SGT, p. 110).

Athena's seduction takes place in fall, and the machinations of the prioress in regard to this seduction are undoubtedly inspired by the fact that she is possessed by the monkey. The monkey is roaming the forest, and it is his eyes that Boris sees glinting in the night.

The prioress scratches herself daintily during the supper; she nibbles cloves from the home of the monkey, Zanzibar; her eyes are "glinting" too; and she frequently speaks of animals shut up in cages. Boris thinks in a corresponding manner of "the dumb struggles within the narrow and wooden chests of old women, sealed up by the Salomonic wax of their education" (SGT, pp. 136-37). During the transformation scene, she behaves like a monkey, jumping about the room wildly until she actually becomes a monkey; and the monkey outside becomes the prioress, "the true Prioress of Closter Seven," of a deportment that is "quietly dignified and kindly as the young people had always remembered it" (SGT, p. 162).

The hero of the tale, Boris von Schreckenstein, possesses most of the qualities termed decadent by Holbrook Jackson in his study of the decadent authors of the "Yellow Book" era: perversity, artificiality, egoism, and curiosity.[4]

Boris is a melancholy egotist. He is saddened by the fact that his desires dissipate before there is time for their fulfillment (SGT, p. 116). Solitude "is always a pleasure to him," and when alone he meditates, significantly enough, "upon the subject of change," feeling that change is "sad" (SGT, pp. 119-22).

Artificiality is the keynote of his existence. Boris is always playing a role, always acting: "To him the theater was real life," it is said, and "as an actor he was his true self, and as soon as he could see a situation in the light of the theater, he would feel at home in it" (SGT, pp. 140-41). With Athena he "accentuates the sweetness and sadness of his behavior" (SGT, p. 142).

Boris is also a rather perverse figure. At the court he has become involved in homosexual circles. Now the prioress is trying to salvage his reputation by quickly marrying him off to Athena of Hopballehus. Knowing that Athena will not quietly and willingly consent to marry Boris, she prepares (also in the best decadent manner) a supper, during the course of which Athena is liberally plied with wine. In order to bolster the courage of Boris, who, in effect, must rape Athena, he is given an aphrodisiac.

As Boris watches Athena at the dining table, he ponders the relationship between beauty and death. He lets "a fantasy take hold of his mind": "He thought that she must have a lovely, an exquisitely beautiful, skeleton. She would lie in the ground like a piece of matchless lace, a work of art in ivory, and in a hundred years might be dug up and turn the heads of old archeologists" (SGT, p. 146). He feels "he might even fall in love with her, could he have her in her beautiful bones alone," and feels "many human relations . . . would be infinitely easier if they could be carried out in the bones only" (SGT, p. 146). On the next morning Athena seems to him "to be well on her way to that purified state of the skeleton in which he had imagined her on the night before. She had in reality a death's-head upon her strong shoulders" (SGT, p. 156).

Athena is innocence pursued, but she differs somewhat from the usual Gothic heroine in that she is too conscious of herself as a Diana, a fanatic virgin, and is very strong of physique. To Boris she looks "like a sturdy young sailor boy about to swab the deck" (SGT, p. 152). However, she is highly innocent, and is, of course, taken advantage of in a rough manner.

"The Monkey" is certainly an orthodox Gothic tale, but though it seems to be mere pastiche it is more than that. The Gothic romance had only one motivation: to thrill and to entertain the reader by providing him with certain spine-chilling sensations. Isak Dinesen employs the tradition of the Gothic romance in a different fashion.

The Gothic tales of Dinesen deal with individuals who are trapped in one way or another, by sex, by class, by history. They deal with people who are imprisoned and long to be set free, to escape. For this reason it is not surprising that exoticism is a central motif in "The Monkey." It is present in the desire of the prioress to surround herself with strange and unusual animals from all parts of the world, and particularly with a monkey from Zanzibar. The very name, "Zanzibar," seems to place her in a state of "gentle melancholy" (SGT, p. 146). Her concern with animals in cages seems to be bound up with unfulfilled desires. The prioress herself is like an animal trapped in a cage, and she longs for freedom.

As a motto for some of these Gothic tales one could use a few lines which Dinesen herself used for *The Angelic Avengers*: "You serious people must not be too hard on human beings for what they choose to amuse themselves with when they are shut up as in a prison, and are not even allowed to say that they are prisoners. If I do not soon get a little bit of fun, I shall die."[5] The Gothic tales of Isak Dinesen seem to fulfill such a need for amusement, but they also deal with people who have such a need, and they do so in a manner that reveals a strong feeling on behalf of the author for those who are trapped by life, particularly for women who are forced by social conventions to live on the edge of life. The two sisters in "The Supper at Elsinore" are predestined to be old maids. The young Childerique in "The Caryatids" does not want to be a caryatid, "always holding up great big stone-houses": her love of danger, her toying with magic and witchcraft, are signs of rebellion against her fate. The prioress in "The Monkey" wants to escape from her prison. Very significant also is the prevalence of bird images in these tales, suggesting the idea of flight and escape. Isak Dinesen, like Elishama Levinsky in "The Immortal Story," has always felt "sympathy and compassion" toward women and birds (AD, p. 229).

Underlying Dinesen's Gothic tales there seems to be a strong personal fear of a too narrow world, a fear of a very fundamental nature. It was probably this fear which sent Dinesen off to Kenya, as it was this fear that sent her father off in search of adventure and excitement. The fear of a life of routine is characteristic of the Dinesen family, all the members of which seem to have high regard for the sailors, soldiers, explorers, adventurers, and vagabonds of this world. The Gothic tales express this feeling, and since they do they cannot be said to be mere pastiche.

In "The Caryatids" one of the favorite Gothic motifs is used: the incest motif. The Gothic novelists were undoubtedly fond of this motif because it was an efficient way of evoking feelings of horror in the reader.

The setting of the tale is Gothic: the fantastic water mill in which the young Childerique is introduced to magic and witchcraft. The place is dangerous and evil, compared to "a viper's nest" (LT, p. 139). Walking into the mill, Childerique feels "the fatality of this one step which took her from the daylight of her life till now into the play with unknown powers" (LT, p. 143).

Childerique is the decadent heroine of "The Caryatids." Like the women in the tales of Barbey d'Aurevilly she is "athirst for mystery, for the impossible, for darkness." [6] The motive for her going to the mill is curiosity, and also "her love of danger. The unknown called her. And she would now know more of witchcraft" (LT, p. 143). The visions in the mill leave her "enraptured and transported," with a "deep ecstasy about this new world opened to her" (LT, p. 146).

Mixed feelings of pleasure and horror are her reactions to the gypsy woman in the mill. When she approaches the mill she feels a deadly nausea at the thought of touching the woman, "as if she had had a snake in front of her" (LT, p. 138).

To the people about her Childerique is strange. She not only wants to "try the taste of poison" and "sleep in the woods at night," she embraces her brother and tells him that she can open up a new world to him: "Oh, I can teach you dances too, darkness, magic too" (LT, pp. 132-35). But the boy is frightened and tells her that she acts like Simkie, the gypsy woman he loves. To Phillip, her husband, Childerique sometimes appears as one of those "deities with hair of snakes" (LT, p. 130).

While Childerique goes to the water mill her husband rummages in the attic and finds the letter which informs him of the fact that Childerique is his sister, and that they have committed incest. The curse laid upon Childerique's father by the gypsy woman's father has been fulfilled. As he realizes the implications of the letter, Phillip is "struck by a great wave of terror," "frightened to death," and feels that he could not suffer "her to think with horror of his embraces" (LT, pp. 125-26).

Childerique is the fatal woman of the decadent tale. The mysterious mill, with its visions, its darkness, its hidden powers, is the exotic element that embodies her real longings

61

and desires. She does not want to be a caryatid, a lady of stone, holding up great stone houses.

"The Supper at Elsinore" is also a Gothic tale. The setting is Elsinore, and since the name of this town invariably makes the reader think of *Hamlet*, it is eminently suitable for three such melancholy figures as the two sisters De Coninck and their brother Morten. They all suffer from this disease that is felt to be a curse on the family.

During the Napoleonic wars, Morten was in charge of a privateer. After the end of the wars he became a pirate, and was finally hanged in the East Indies. The story tells of his reappearance at Elsinore, no fewer than seven times. At the news of his reappearance the two sisters feel "their hair stand on end" (SGT, p. 246).

Morten was once engaged to marry a girl in Elsinore, but left before the wedding and spent the rest of his life at sea. He has led an adventurous life. The sisters envy him this exciting existence. Like wild animals imprisoned in cages, having been predestined to become old maids, they long for the freedom he has had. They are dissatisfied: when Morten leaves on the stroke of midnight Eliza calls out: "You! You have been to these great warm seas of which you talk, to a hundred countries. You have been married to five people" (SGT, p. 269). Eliza's whole existence has been one of longing, longing for adventure, for foreign lands. As already mentioned, bird images are common in the tale, and this is probably due to the fact that the two sisters are represented as trapped human beings who wish to escape from their "cages."

Thus Morten De Coninck's engagement to Adrienne Rosenstand is described as one of "the falcon to the white dove." She is not "a young eagle bride," a fitting mate for a hero, but "a little *bourgeoise*, an ornamental bird out of the poultry yard of Elsinore" (SGT, p. 228). For this reason Morten cannot marry her. Eliza De Coninck is called "The Swan of Elsinore," and moves with pride and lightness "like an old Arab mare a little stiff, but unmistakably noble, at ease in the sphere of war and fantasias" (SGT, pp. 243-44). In her heart is "a great, mad, wing-clipped bird, fluttering in the winter sunset," and she can see her own large nose, "pink under her veil like a terrible, cruel beak" (SGT, p. 250). The two sisters feel that they look like a pair of old scarecrows, but Morten says that Fanny, his sister, looks like "a bumblebee-hawk-moth," and if they, his sisters, did look like old ladies he would not mind, because "when grandmamma had her birthday parties at Øregaard, that was where you would see a houseful of fine old ladies. Like a grand aviary, and grandmamma amongst them like a proud cockatoo" (SGT, p. 256).

There are also a few Gothic elements in "The Dreamers." The fantastic Alpine setting has already been mentioned. The terror of Olalla is reflected in the snow and the winds and the wildness of the elements. There is a wild winter moon watching the melodramatic coach-ride into the pass.

The story of Pellegrina Leoni centers around the mask motif, which will be considered in the next chapter. The mask motif as such does not seem to be a common Gothic motif, but in this tale we encounter a variant of it which might be considered Gothic: Pellegrina has no shadow. She is a female Peter Schlemihl, and Marcus Cocoza has taken over the role of her shadow. Her shadow is her true self: thus "The Dreamers," too, deals with a character who wishes to escape.

As in "The Supper at Elsinore," the escape motif is suggested by bird images. Pellegrina has, in addition, some of the qualities of the fatal woman, of a Childerique, an aspect of the tale suggested by the snake imagery.

Olalla, Pellegrina's first mask, has a long scar from a burn running from her left ear to her collar bone "like a little white snake." She is also compared to "a tame lioness, strong of tooth and claw, insinuating herself into your favor" (SGT, pp. 285-86). As Madame Rosalba "she is a swan in the lake of life everlasting" (SGT, p. 305). Fleeing in the snowstorm, Olalla sometimes looked "like an angry owl on a branch, her wings spread out," and at other times "she was like a crane when it runs along the ground to catch the wind and get on the wing" (SGT, p. 319). Looking into her face is like looking into the face of a falcon (SGT, p, 321). Throwing herself over the cliffs, she "behaved exactly like a black martin when you see it throw itself out from a slope or a roof to get off the ground and take flight" (SGT, p. 327). To Marcus Cocoza, Pellegrina appeared as "a winged lioness" and as "a young shark in the sea, mastering the strong green water by a stroke of her fins, thus did she swim along within the depths and mysteries of the great world" (SGT, p. 332). In her life she was, says Marcus, "like a great bird, an albatross, asked to hop and twitter with the little birds within an aviary" (SGT, p. 336). While most people appear to Cocoza as "little vipers or scorpions," Pellegrina Leoni is not a "venomous snake, but a python": "Very often," he used to say to her, "in your walk you recall to me the dancing snakes which I was once shown by an Indian snake-charmer. But you have no poison whatever in you, and if you kill it is by the force of your embrace" (SGT, p. 337).

In several of the *Seven Gothic Tales* Dinesen introduces decadent figures in stories that center around motifs of a non-Gothic nature, thus making use of the Gothic tradition for her own purposes.

Count Augustus von Schimmelmann, the young Dane in "The Roads Round Pisa," is such a decadent version of the Hamlet figure, incapable of action, pondering the problem of truth, searching for his own identity in his little pocket mirror. In contrast to the Italians, who are passionately committed to a life of action, von Schimmelmann is a melancholiac. Like Stendhal, Dinesen points to the great gulf between the melancholy North and the passionate South.

In "The Poet" von Schimmelmann has grown older. He is an esthete, a connoisseur of the arts, but not a creative artist. He has taken to drugs, hashish in particular. His concern with form, his interest in young men, his gradual decay, and his aristocratic background are qualities which bring to mind another visitor to Italy from the North, Thomas Mann's Gustav von Aschenbach.

Gustav von Aschenbach was of course to some extent patterned on the German Romantic poet Count August von Platen (1796-1835). In "The Deluge at Norderney" we meet von Platen in the guise of Count Seraphina, who is Des Esseintes, Ludwig II, and von Platen rolled into one. Living at the romantic old castle of Angelshorn, he surrounds himself with young boys. With them he sometimes drinks wine out of a skull, "to keep present the thought of death and eternity," but taking care that "it should not be the skull of a lady" (SGT, pp. 44-45).

A common figure in a number of Dinesen's tales is the diabolic old man, the villain of the cruel tale.

In "The Roads Round Pisa" the impotent Prince Pozentiani hires a *bravo*, Prince Giovanni, to help him consummate his marriage to Rosina, and is foiled by the fact that Agnese takes Rosina's place on the wedding night.

In "The Poet" Councilor Mathiesen treats Anders and the dancer Fransine like two marionettes, plays with their youth and love, until he is shot by Anders and stoned by Fransine.

In "The Immortal Story" the rich old Mr. Clay in Canton gets the whim of making an old sailor's story come true. To this effect he stages a comedy, toying with the lives of an unknown Danish sailor and a young actress. Like the marionettes in several of Dinesen's tales, they do not, however, become victims of his machinations: by playing their roles to the hilt they are transformed and come to re-enact the old story of Paul and Virginie.

If any one of Dinesen's works deserves the label "mere pastiche," it is probably the novel *The Angelic Avengers*.

The novel is, as Hans Brix has shown, a pastiche of the sentimental English novel of the early nineteenth century.[7] The events in the first chapter are quite similar to those in Charlotte Brontë's *Jane Eyre* of 1847. Lucan Bellenden, like Jane Eyre, is a young orphan girl who takes a position as a governess. The crisis occurs when the father of the children proposes that the girl become his mistress. In both cases the girls flee.

The action in Dinesen's novel takes place in England in the fall and summer of 1841. Because of the irony involved in the story, *The Angelic Avengers* resembles Jane Austen's *Northanger Abbey*. Lucan finds her friend Zozine, whose father has left the country because of economic difficulties. Both are eighteen years old. Left to their own resources, the girls take a position with a retired reverend, a man named Pennhallow, who brings them to his house in Languedoc. A kind old gentleman, he teaches them history and the classics. Soon they realize, through a mysterious letter, that their benfactor is, in fact, a white slave trader, in the habit of bringing unsuspecting young ladies to his farm.

The Gothic character of the novel now emerges clearly. Lucan and Zozine are the persecuted young maidens. The Reverend Pennhallow is a diabolic Dr. Jekyll and Mr. Hyde. An incest motif is introduced when it is discovered that Pennhallow is married to his sister.

The novel is exciting to read, and its gentle spoofing makes it a sophisticated piece of entertainment. But it is undoubtedly a mere entertainment. The escape motif, so meaningful in Dinesen's Gothic tales, in "The Monkey" and in "The Caryatids," is here introduced only in order to produce an element of suspense. The prioress and Childerique were trying to escape from the bonds of a too narrow world; Lucan and Zozine are only running away from a wicked old man. The incest motif, too, lacks the significance it possessed in "The Caryatids." The novel also lacks the historical context of Jane Austen's *Northanger Abbey*. The ironies and gentle spoofings of the latter acquire most of their meaning from the fact that Jane Austen was parodying the clearly defined tradition of the Gothic novel which her contemporaries were involved in. Dinesen's novel, lacking such historical significance, is mere pastiche.

3

THE
MASK

THE TALES woven around the motif of the mask are in many ways very similar to the Gothic tales. They express the same basic theme, a central one in Dinesen's view of life: the need for a life of adventure, freedom, and imagination felt by those who for one reason or another are trapped, are unable to experience life fully. The differences between the two kinds of tales are due to the fact that the tales built around the mask motif project and explore this essentially Romantic philosophy of life in a more conscious and deliberate manner. They deal, in addition, with a central problem in Dinesen's works: the problem of illusion.

Those who have met Karen Blixen in person have hardly ever failed to comment on her histrionic personality.[1] She loves the theater and the opera: the worlds of Shakespeare and Mozart.[2] She has a great fondness for the grand gesture and the well-formulated repartee. To judge from the number of references to Haroun al

68

Raschid scattered throughout the tales, he seems to be the monarch she admires above all others. Like Henri Beyle and Søren Kierkegaard, two "romantic psychologists" with whom she has much in common, Blixen surrounds herself with pseudonyms. Stendhal and Henri Brulard; Frater Taciturnus and Johannes Silentius; Isak Dinesen, Pierre Andrézel, and Osceola; these are the masks of singularly histrionic personalities. It is hardly surprising to find, then, that the motif of the mask is a central one in Dinesen's tales.

In view of her own histrionic personality, and of her interest in the problem of illusion, it is not surprising that more than half of the figures that move through the tales are artists, or involved with the arts in some way. It is only natural that a writer for whom life is art, and art is life, should surround herself with figures who are by their very profession playing roles, donning and doffing masks.

Pellegrina Leoni, her pupil Emmanuele, Jonathan Maersk, Achille Papin, Martina and Filippa, Giovanni Ferrer, and Nathalie are singers. Leonidas and his pupil Angelo are sculptors. Mira Jama, Count Seraphina, Charlie Despard, Anders Kube, Councilor Mathiesen are storytellers or poets. Pino Pizzuti operates a marionette theater, and Marcus Cocoza a ballet company. Old Soerensen is a theater director. Agnese and Jens Jespersen write plays. Boris von Schreckenstein and Kasparson are actors. Virginie and Malli Ross are actresses. Alkmene, Heloise, Fransine, and Thusmu are dancers. A few of the figures are real, living artists of the time: Henrik Ibsen in "The Pearl"; the eighteenth-century Danish poet and playwright Johannes Ewald in "Converse at Night"; and Ludwig von Platen, as Count Seraphina, in "The Deluge at Norderney."

Many of the figures in the tales are aware of the fact that they are playing a role in some kind of story or drama. In line with the demands of the role they must also be willing to undergo the transformations that the role requires. For this reason we find the figures in a perpetual state of metamorphosis. They change their physical appearance; they change their social roles; they change their sex; they change into animals; and they change into mythical beings.

Some of the changes of physical appearance, of expression and gesture, under the influence of passion or tension, have already been indicated.

The change of sex is frequent enough to be quite remarkable. Calypso is brought up as a boy and is going to chop off her breasts in order to become more like one when she discovers that she is really a woman and, as such, desirable. The bald old man in "The Roads Round Pisa" is suddenly transformed into a fine old lady of imposing appearance. Agnese in the same tale dresses and looks like a boy (she looks like Lord Byron!), and von Schimmelmann is quite embarrassed to discover that she is really a woman.

The prioress in "The Monkey" is transformed into a monkey, but regains her original appearance after a period of time. The old Lapp woman plays a falcon in "The Sailor-Boy's Tale." In addition, a number of characters are, as indicated above, compared to animals in terms of physical appearance or behavior.

Many of the characters change their social roles. Nasrud-Din, the Oriental prince in "A Consolatory Tale," disguises himself as a beggar like his famous countryman Haroun al Raschid. Mizzi and Lotti in "The Invincible Slaveowners" try to keep up appearances by taking turns at playing the servant and governess of each other. Axel Leth disguises himself as their servant. Heloise, the Paris music-hall dancer whose daily job is to undress in public, plays a highly respectable widow in "The Heroine," becoming a heroine precisely through an incident in which she refuses to undress before a German colonel. Countess Sophie, Childerique's mother in "The Caryatids," is said to have a "curious taste for disguise, so that she would, like a neat female Haroun al Raschid, become acquainted with the poor and outcast of the land in her maid's apron, or even dressed up as a horse-dealer's boy" (LT, p. 121). In "The Roads Round Pisa" Rosina and Agnese change roles for Rosina's wedding night. In "The Cloak" Angelos and Leonidas change roles: Angelos takes Leonidas' place in the prison while Leonidas goes to see his wife on the night when Angelos was going to see her!

All these changes seem, however, to be primarily technical devices. As such they are frequently employed in fantastic tales. They are integral elements in the author's attempt to create a world in which everything is possible.

If we now turn our attention from the use of metamorphosis as a literary method to the use of it as a philosophy of life, we must first examine the two tales which clearly embody this mask philosophy: "The Deluge at Norderney" and "The Dreamers." Both of these tales have, significantly enough, an actor and an opera singer among their central figures.

The theme of role-playing is introduced at the very beginning of "The Deluge at Norderney" as the characters pass in review. Miss Nat-og-Dag is a lady of the strictest virtue, and always has been, but in her imagination she has projected herself in another role: she believes herself to be one of the greatest sinners of her age, and has a great faith in a past of "colossal licentiousness" (SGT, p. 21). This is her great role.

The mask motif is introduced by Miss Nat-og-Dag in her conversation with Kasparson. "Where in all the world," she says, "did you get the idea that the Lord wants the truth from us? . . . Why, he knows it already, and may even have

found it a little bit dull. Truth is for tailors and shoemakers"
(SGT, p. 24). The Lord, on the other hand, she continues,
"has a penchant for masquerades," a tendency he showed in
"masquerading pretty freely when he took on flesh and dwelt
amongst us." The nearest to the spirit of God is the monarch
Haroun al Raschid, who also had "a taste for disguise" (SGT,
p. 25). From his behavior a lesson is to be learned, a lesson
which she has given to her many admirers: "Make poetry . . .
use your imagination, disguise the truth to me. Your truth
comes out quite early enough . . . and that is the end of the
game" (SGT, p. 25).

Kasparson adds the observation that the mask is not all
deception in that it reveals something of the spirit or heart
of the player, something which the conventions of life con-
ceal. For this reason the Lord, "the Arbiter of the masquerade,"
might say, "By thy mask I shall know thee." Kasparson also
adds the ingenious notion that the day of judgment will not
be the day on which the Lord will unveil "our own poor little
attempts at deceit, about which the Lord does indeed already
know all," but will be the hour when the Lord "himself lets
fall the mask" (SGT, p. 26).

In the second conversation between the valet and Miss
Nat-og-Dag the theme of the mask is further developed. Since
the person will be known by the mask he dons, the greatness
of the role he plays will depend on the greatness of his imagination. In the modern world, Kasparson laments, in the
modern world of Louis Philippe and the bourgeoisie, this
greatness of the imagination is, however, sadly lacking. He
fears that we are now ruled by an inferior dynasty of heaven,
as we are ruled by an inferior dynasty on earth. What is
lacking is the quality of charlatanry indispensable for a great
artist. "Madame," says Kasparson,

to my mind there never was a great artist who was not a bit of a charlatan; nor a great king, nor a god. The quality of charlatanry is indispensable in a court, or a theater, or in paradise. Thunder and lightning, the new moon, a nightingale, a young girl—all these are bits of charlatanry, of a divine swank. So is the *gallérie de glaces* at Versailles. But King Louis Philippe has no drop of blood of the charlatan in him; he is genuinely reliable all through [SGT, pp. 58-59].

There follows the parable "The Wine of the Tetrarch," and the scene in which the Cardinal is unmasked, and we learn that Kasparson's face is hidden under the bandages. His reasons for playing the role of the Cardinal are partly given in the moral of the parable ("There are things worse than perdition"), and partly in the ensuing conversation.

Kasparson has been a man of many professions: barber, ballet dancer, printer of revolutionary papers, courtesan, valet, but basically and foremost an actor. As an actor he has always wanted an opportunity to play a great role. In addition, he is a bastard son of the Duke of Orléans and very proud. "The moment," says Kasparson, "in which I killed the Cardinal, that was the mating of my soul with destiny." "I told you," he says, "I am an actor. Shall not an actor have a role?" The only question to be asked is: was his playing a success or a fiasco? "I have played the part well," he asserts, "the Cardinal would have applauded me, for he was a fine connoisseur of the art." And he adds:

The only thing . . . which he might have criticized is this: he might have held that I overdid my rôle. . . . But in any case . . . at the day of judgment God shall not say to me now: "Kasparson, you bad actor! How was it that you could not, not even with death in your own heart, play me the dying Gaul?" [SGT, pp. 74-75].

Miss Nat-og-Dag's further question as to why he wanted this particular role so much, Kasparson answers by saying that he has within him the arrogant blood of a bastard, full of vanity, claiming splendor. Thus he had to see once the fishermen and peasants worship him as they worshiped the Cardinal:

> If they would have made me their master I would have served them all my life. If they would only have fallen down and worshipped me, I would have died for them. But they would not. That they reserved for the Cardinal. Only tonight have they come around. They have seen the face of God in my face. They will tell you, after tonight, that there was a white light over the boat in which I went out with them [SGT, pp. 75-76].

Now he has played his role, and feels he has played it well. He is right: his name lives on, and he becomes a mythical figure.

As presented in "The Deluge at Norderney" the philosophy of the mask is both aristocratic and Romantic. It is both an attitude toward life and a conception of art and the artist.

In Miss Nat-og-Dag's opening statement the truth was said to be for "tailors and shoemakers," for the bourgeoisie. It so happens that there is a young representative of this class on the hayloft, Jonathan Maersk. A singer by profession, and a favorite of the Baron Joachim Gersdorff in Copenhagen, he has been one of the most popular young men in fashionable society. However, when he lost his voice he made a discovery which has made him into the fashionable melancholy man: he discovered that people acclaimed him as a singer even when he had lost his voice, because he was Baron Gersdorff's favorite. He is shocked at the deceit and sham of the world of fashion.

Jonathan is also an artist, or was one, but he differs from the actor Kasparson in that he wants the truth, while Kasparson's motto is: "Disguise yourselves." Jonathan's attitude to this philosophy is typically bourgeois; like King Louis Philippe he has not the indispensable quality of great charlatanry: a great imagination. Kasparson's philosophy asserts that reality is a creation of the imagination, and that one shall be judged by his mask, that is, by the range of his imagination. This attitude toward life is aristocratic because it emphasizes passion, courage, energy, and imagination and leads to an acceptance and affirmation of destiny. Jonathan's attitude is bourgeois because it dwells on the problem of the relationship between appearance and reality and develops into melancholy because of the discrepancy between the two. Jonathan, like Augustus von Schimmelmann, looks into the mirror and wonders about his true identity, thus turning into the melancholy man made fashionable at this time by Chateaubriand, Byron, and Musset. Kasparson also watches the mirror, but like an actor, considering which mask to don, he chooses a role and plays it to the hilt. The mask is the destiny which man chooses for himself.

Dinesen's statement of the aristocratic philosophy of the mask bears a striking resemblance to that of William Butler Yeats, the Irish playwright and poet, also a great histrionic personality in his own right. Yeats did, of course, develop his philosophy of the mask on a much more elaborate scale: as a central theme in his later poetic dramas it is demonstrated at length and examined in detail. But in its most concentrated statement it is identical to Isak Dinesen's. Yeats felt that our modern culture "with its doctrine of sincerity and self-realization" had made us gentle and passive. By being true to ourselves we had achieved nothing since our "selves" were so insignificant. The Middle Ages and the Renaissance, on the other hand, founded their ideal behavior on the concept of the mask: the men of those ages imitated Christ, or some classic hero. Thus they achieved greatness. "St. Francis and Caesar Borgia," says Yeats, "made themselves over-mastering, creative persons by turning from the mirror to meditation upon a mask. When I had this thought I could see nothing else in life." [3]

This aristocratic view of life places a high value on the imagination. For this reason it is intimately related to the Romantic conception of art and the artist. The artist, too, is different from the bourgeois. He is a charlatan, a masked player, and thus highly unreliable from the bourgeois point of view. This conception of art and the artist bears a striking similarity to Thomas Mann's in his early stories as well as in his later novels.[4] The artist is a confidence man because he does not mirror reality; he transforms it, or re-creates it, in his imagination. The greatness of his art depends on the courage and the range of his imagination. Speaking of the courage of the Creator as manifested in his arrangements of the matters of love and marriage, Kasparson says: "What an overwhelming lesson to all artists! Be not afraid of absurdity; do not shrink from the fantastic. Within a dilemma, choose the most unheard-of, the most dangerous solution. Be brave, be brave!" (SGT, p. 55).

The same philosophy of art and the artist is presented in "The Dreamers," also a tale of the mask. The story, narrated by an Englishman, Lincoln Forsner, on board a ship traveling from Lamu to Zanzibar, concerns a certain famous Italian opera singer, Pellegrina Leoni, who lost her voice in a fire. Having lost her voice, she proceeds to disguise herself. Lincoln knows her as Olalla, a prostitute in a Roman brothel. During his pursuit of Olalla, Lincoln meets two gentlemen, Friedrich Hohenemser and Baron Guildenstern, who are also acquainted with Pellegrina. Hohenemser knows her as Madame Lola, a maker of bonnets in Switzerland, and a revolutionary who persuaded him to assassinate the Bishop of St. Gallen. The Baron knows her as Madame Rosalba, a lady who is something of a saint. When she enters the Alpine inn where all these gentlemen have gathered, she is a Frau Councilor Heerbrand.

Pellegrina Leoni had always been disturbed by the fact that the "phenomena of life were not great enough for her," that "they were not in proportion with her own heart." In this respect, says Marcus Cocoza, she was a Donna Quixotta de la Mancha. "She was badly hurt and disappointed," he says, "because the world was not a much greater place than it is, and because nothing more colossal, more like the dramas of the stage, took place in it, not even when she herself went into the show with all her might" (SGT, p. 336).

Then disaster: she loses her voice. In despair Pellegrina seeks to take her own life. Her friend Marcus seeks to reawaken her interest in life by telling her of a ballet that he is planning to write about the things that have befallen the two of them. She listens attentively to him, and a couple of days later she sends for Marcus and tells him of her plan.

Pellegrina has come to the realization that she has always been thinking only of Pellegrina. Now Pellegrina shall be buried forever because to be one person, and one person only, is to suffer. She will be many women and the moment she begins to think very much of what happens to one of them she will go away at once. "I will not be one person again, Marcus, I will be always many persons from now." She tells Marcus to do the same:

> Be many people. Give up this game of being one and of being always Marcus Cocoza. You have worried too much about Marcus Cocoza, so that you have been really his slave and his prisoner. . . . I feel, Marcus—I am sure—that all people in the world ought to be, each of them, more than one, and they would all, yes, all of them, be more easy at heart. They would have a little fun [SGT, p. 345].

77

From this time on Pellegrina leads an exciting life. She is no longer worried about Pellegrina; consequently she knows neither care nor fear, neither regret nor ambition. She has no self and no shadow but the mysterious Cocoza who follows her about. Her adventures are finally as extravagant and as colossal as the dramas on the stage. She might, in effect, be said to be acting all the various roles in Cocoza's ballet *Philomela*.

The last act of this adventure (and Dinesen presents it, in effect, as a final scene in a ballet) is the unmasking of Pellegrina and her consequent death. Her three pursuers are told that they have courted the same woman.

The meaning of the tale is suggested by an image. The storyteller, Mira Jama, says that he no longer tells tales because he has lost his capacity to fear, and "when you know what things are really like, you can make no poems about them." "I have become too familiar with life," he says, "it can no longer delude me into believing that one thing is much worse than the other." So he dreams, because in his dreams he knows fear. In order to illustrate what he means he uses the image of the coffee tree:

> You know, Tembu . . . that if, in planting a coffee tree, you bend the taproot, that tree will start, after a little time, to put out a multitude of small delicate roots near the surface. That tree will never thrive, nor bear fruit, but it will flower more richly than the others.
>
> Those fine roots are the dreams of the tree. As it puts them out, it need no longer think of its bent taproot. It keeps alive by them— a little, not very long. Or you can say that it dies by them, if you like. For really, dreaming is the well-mannered people's way of committing suicide [SGT, p. 277].

Pellegrina taught Lincoln how to dream. She wanted to forget her taproot, and she succeeded by putting out a number of small taproots, her dreams, all the roles she played in order to disguise herself. When she was unmasked she died. This seems to suggest that the mask is a value conferred by the imagination on reality. When exposed, reality is deadly. Only through the application of the mask, or several of them, does life become exciting and meaningful, only then does one thing become more important than any other. Mira Jama says that his familiarity with life has made it impossible for him to believe "that one thing is much worse than the other."

Even Friedrich Hohenemser succeeded in freeing himself from his taproot. He had spent his whole life trying to prove to others that he had a taproot; that he, Friedrich Hohenemser, really existed. The trouble with him, says Lincoln, was that he

> . . . had no imagination, and was, besides, very honest. He could invent nothing for himself, but was left to describe such preferences as he really found in his own mind, which were always preciously few. Probably it was, altogether, his lack of imagination which prevented him from existing. For if you will create, as you know [Lincoln addresses Mira Jama], you must first imagine, and as he could not imagine what Friedrich Hohenemser was to be like, he failed to produce any Friedrich Hohenemser at all [SGT, p. 293].

However, after his experience with Pellegrina he withdrew "from the hard and hopeless task of being Friedrich Hohenemser and took on the existence of a small landowner in a far district, by the name of Fridolin Emser," and he became very happy (SGT, p. 348).

The mask philosophy as presented in "The Dreamers" is a Romantic philosophy of art and life because it places a very high value on illusion and dreams, maintaining that reality is mean and inferior. The Romantic artist is the artist of the mask, because he projects a world in which all is possible, and over which he has unlimited power because he has, as an artist, unlimited freedom to transform it. As such he is also the representative on earth of the greatest mask artist of them all: God. "I have been trying for a long time to understand God," says Mira Jama.

> Now I have made friends with him. To love him truly you must love change, and you must love a joke, these being the true inclinations of his own heart. Soon I shall take to loving a joke so well that I, who once turned the blood of all the world to ice, shall become a teller of funny tales, to make people laugh [SGT, p. 355].

A deep and fundamental skepticism lies at the basis of this view of art and life.

4

MARIONETTE
AND
MYTH

I HAVE ALREADY commented on the fact that in many instances Dinesen's figures appear and act like marionettes. I have also suggested (as have Harald Nielsen and Aage Henriksen) that this manner of rendering character is more than just a technical device: it is a view of life.[1] The marionette motif is, in fact, a very basic and central one in Dinesen's tales. This indicates that the author looks at life as a kind of marionette play in which human beings are the puppets and God is the great puppeteer.

The first appearance of the marionette motif is in a little play which Dinesen published in 1926. It is entitled *The Revenge of Truth*, and it is a marionette comedy.[2] This play is important because it was later to form the central core of the marionette tale "The Roads Round Pisa." In that tale the little play is referred to as "the immortal *Revenge of Truth*, that most charming of marionette comedies" (SGT, p. 198). Its plot is created by a witch who pronounces "upon the house wherein all the characters are collected, a curse, to the effect that any lie told within it will become true" (SGT, p. 198). The moral of the play is stated by the witch at the end of the performance:

> The truth, my children, is that we are, all of us, acting in a marionette comedy. What is important more than anything else in a marionette comedy, is keeping the ideas of the author clear. This is the real happiness of life, and now that I have at last come into a marionette play, I will never go out of it again. But you, my fellow actors, keep the ideas of the author clear. Aye, drive them to their utmost consequences [SGT, p. 199].

In "The Roads Round Pisa" the little play is attended by the company gathered at the inn, and Count Augustus von Schimmelmann, in particular, is struck by the moral of this play, which seems to him suddenly to hold a lot of truth: "Yes, he thought, if my life were only a marionette comedy in which I had my part and knew it well, then it might be very easy and sweet. . . . If I have now at last, he thought, come into a marionette play, I will not go out of it again" (SGT, p. 199).

Count Augustus has, in fact, come into a marionette play, though the role he plays in it is not a great one. It is the other figures in the tale who are like the little actors in the play. They are the figures on whom truth has its revenge, because they have not kept "the ideas of the author clear." Several of the characters in the tale have fought against their destiny and are to be punished. The old Countess Carlotta has tampered with the destiny intended for her niece, Rosina, by attempting to marry her off to the impotent Prince Pozentiani. Prince Pozentiani has tampered with destiny by sending his *bravo*, Prince Nino, to consummate the marriage for him. Rosina has acted as God's instrument unknowingly by sending her girl friend, Agnese, to take her place during the wedding night. Those who have tried to obstruct the idyl, as Henriksen puts it, are transformed into fools after the author has been compelled to make the idyl into a complicated comedy of intrigue. They suddenly realize that a kind of providence has transformed them from "villains in a human tragedy to fools in a divine comedy." [3] The old countess realizes:

> If I had been shown this child from the beginning I should have been docile and have let the Lord ride me in any direction he wanted. Life is a mosaic work of the Lord's, which he keeps filling in bit by bit. If I had seen this little bit of bright color as the centerpiece, I would have understood the pattern, and would not have shaken it all to pieces so many times, and given the good Lord so much trouble in putting it together again [SGT, p. 215].

Henriksen has pointed to a definite affinity between Heinrich von Kleist's little dialogue about the marionette theater and Dinesen's ideas as expressed in "The Roads Round Pisa." [4] The central notion in Kleist's dialogue, Henriksen maintains, is that each person has a certain destiny, but that man, unlike the marionette figure, has the doubtful privilege of being able to struggle against his destiny, and to try to form himself according to his own desires. Henriksen quotes a passage from *Out of Africa* which expresses the same idea:

> Pride is faith in the idea that God had, when he made us. A proud man is conscious of the idea, and aspires to realize it. He does not strive towards a happiness, or comfort, which may be irrelevant to God's idea of him. His success is the idea of God, successfully carried through, and he is in love with his destiny. . . . People who have no pride are not aware of any idea of God in the making of them, and sometimes they make you doubt that there has ever been much of an idea, or else it has been lost, and who shall find it again? They have got to accept as success what others warrant to be so, and to take their happiness, and even their own selves, at the quotation of the day. They tremble, with reason, before their fate [OA, p. 261].

There are then, it seems, good and bad marionettes. Rosina is a good marionette because she tries to keep the ideas of the author clear. Count Augustus is a "lost" marionette because he has lost his destiny, and has to rely upon others to tell him who he is. The bad marionettes are punished; the good and the lost are rewarded with a sign, an insight in the form of a picture or an image, that they will treasure and remember. Augustus gets a smelling bottle, and he feels that there was in this "decision of fate, something which was meant for him only—a value, a depth, a resort even, in life which belonged to him alone, and which he could not share with anybody else any more than he would be able to share his dreams" (SGT, p. 216). At last he has come into a marionette play.

The tale of Count Augustus is reminiscent of another tale entitled "The Roads of Life," which is included in *Out of Africa*. This is a tale which Dinesen says she was often told as a child, because it was a picture story created before the listener while the tale was being told. The story is about a man who lives in a little round house with a round window and little triangular garden in front of it. Not far from the house is a lake with a lot of fish in it. The man wakes up one night hearing a terrific noise. He sets out to investigate, and the rest of the story is a description of his running back and forth several times, falling into ditches, and so forth. He finds the source of the trouble, repairs the damage, and goes back home to bed. Now, if you trace his wanderings during the night they form a picture, the picture of a stork.

After having told this story Dinesen adds this reflection. The man must have wondered, she says, what was the idea of these trials: "But through them all he kept his purpose in view, nothing made him turn round and go home, he finished his course, he kept his faith. That man had his reward. In the morning he saw the stork. He must have laughed out loud then." And she adds a personal thought: "The tight place, the dark pit in which I am now lying, of what bird is it the talon? When the design of my life is completed, shall I, shall other people see a stork?" (OA, pp. 251-53).

The man in the story has been a good marionette: he has kept the ideas of the author clear and has been rewarded. But his role is not a great one: he is but a fool in a comedy. There are, however, marionettes who are more fortunate in that the roles that they are expected to perform are more meaningful. Dinesen suggests this in a few paragraphs following the reflections quoted above. She says: "Troy in flames, seven years of exile, thirteen good ships lost. What is to come out of it?" She answers: "Unsurpassed elegance, majestic stateliness, and sweet tenderness." Similarly she brings to test the second article of the faith of the Christian Church: "That He was crucified, dead and buried, that He went down into Hell, and also did rise again the third day, that He ascended into Heaven, and from thence shall come again." She asks: "What ups and downs, as terrible as those of the man in the story. What is to come out of all this?" She answers: "The second article of the Creed of half the world" (OA, p. 253).

Here both Ulysses and Christ are looked upon as some kind of marionette figures. They are different from ordinary marionettes in that their roles and their rewards are greater. They are no longer mere marionettes: they have become mythical figures. The myth differs from the marionette comedy in that it is a repetition down through the ages of the valid realizations of destiny. It is as if the author of the world did not possess an unlimited number of equally good ideas, as if he varied the successful themes, used the same patterns in creating new destinies.

In his essay on the marionette motif in Dinesen's works, Aage Henriksen has made an interesting reference to another

contemporary author who has also used extensively the marionette motif in his writing. The reference is, specifically, to
Thomas Mann's essay, *Freud and the Future,* in which Mann
discusses his own novel, *Joseph and His Brothers,* a work
which in his own writing marks a turning away from the
bourgeois-individual life in favor of the mythic-typical life.
The epic structure of the Joseph novels is the re-enacted myth.
The myth is defined as an archetypal experience, forever repeated throughout human history. When the individual realizes that he is re-enacting an archetypal experience he finds a
great happiness, because he comes into contact with patterns
of human experience that are eternally valid. Mann uses examples from history to show how great figures in the moment
of fulfillment grab a quotation to indicate, triumphantly, that
they have now completed a mythical life. Thus Christ's words
on the cross are not original, but a quotation from the Twenty-
second Psalm, which is an announcement of the coming of
Messiah. The quotation means: I am the one who was expected, I am Messiah and lived and died as it was written.
Thus Joseph is happy and calm in success and defeat because
he knows, deep down, that he is playing the main role in an
old play, that he is identical with the Egyptian god who was
torn to pieces, buried, and later raised.

Mann ends his essay by bringing the whole discussion of
the myth back to the marionette play, in which the dolls play
in a certain predetermined pattern. "Under the art optics of
the myth," says Mann, "life appears as such a theatrical fulfillment of something preordained." [5]

Some of Mann's comments are interesting in that they suggest that the marionette philosophy is not necessarily pessi-
mistic. If we compare Dinesen's marionette philosophy with
that of a modern Swedish dramatist such as Hjalmar Bergman, the author of a number of marionette plays (and in

86

many ways perhaps the modern writer who most resembles Dinesen), we find that Bergman's conception is that life laughs at our plans, that we are the victims of change and circumstance.[6] This is the typical marionette philosophy. Dinesen's conception of the marionette comedy of life suggests, on the other hand, the existence of a reasonable plan, that we are in safe hands when we have come into a marionette comedy.

In "The Roads Round Pisa" the bad marionettes are punished, and the good are rewarded. The roles played by the various figures do not, however, have any mythical significance. In some of the other tales the characters do take on a mythical, archetypal role.

"The Immortal Story" is set in Canton in the 1860's and describes the wicked machinations of a rich old tea trader, Mr. Clay. A lover of facts, of real things, he dislikes stories because they are untrue. He gets the idea of making a story come true, the old story of the sailor who is approached by a rich old man who offers him five guineas if he will do him the service of sleeping with his wife and begetting an heir. With the aid of his clerk, Elishama Levinsky, Mr. Clay procures the service of a young lady with a "venturesome past," who, for a price of one hundred guineas, is willing to come into the story, and finish it. A handsome, young Danish sailor is found. Virginie has always wanted to be an actress, she is willing to play the game (her motto is *Pourquoi pas?*), and when the sailor enters her bedroom she plays the seventeen-year-old girl he takes her to be. The boy is also seventeen and very innocent.

Mr. Clay looks at Virginie and the sailor, whose name is Paul, as jumping jacks, pulled by his strong hands. They will, as he puts it, be doing nothing that he has not willed them to do. But like Pozentiani, Mr. Clay is proven wrong. For

Paul and Virginie are, in fact, transformed into the immortal couple. As Paul begins to make love to her, Virginie re-experiences the moment she lost her virginity during an earthquake in Tokyo. She suddenly cries out: "For God's sake! Get up, we must get up. There is an earthquake!—do you not feel the earthquake!" The young sailor answers: "No. No. It is not an earthquake. It is me" (AD, p. 218). Having fulfilled his mission as puppeteer, in the hands of a greater power than his own, Mr. Clay collapses just like Prince Pozentiani in "The Roads Round Pisa."

"Tempests" is also a marionette tale. Herr Soerensen, a Danish theater director with a touring company, comes to Norway. Looking for a young girl to play Ariel in a performance of Shakespeare's drama *The Tempest,* Soerensen decides to employ a certain Malli Ross.

On its way to a coastal town where the play is to be performed, the ship carrying Miss Ross is almost wrecked in a storm but is saved by her heroism. The mate, a certain Ferdinand Skaeret, dies. Malli becomes the center of attention in the town, is introduced into the shipowner's family, and falls in love with the son, Arndt Hosewinckel. The romance between the two of them is broken off in a strange fashion when Malli comes to the realization that she has betrayed all the fine and honest people in the town. She is no heroine, because the bravery she exhibited was due to the fact that during the shipwreck she thought she was performing her role in *The Tempest.* Theater and reality had become one to her.

Old Soerensen plays, of course, the role of Prospero. Like Mr. Clay he is almost a demonic figure, both a shrewd businessman and a devoted artist. A strong man, he wishes to control and to create the world about him. He is the creator of Malli, she is in his hands. She has become Ariel, his servant, and her primary dedication is to art, to Shakespeare, and

88

not to this world. Therefore, she must leave and go with Herr Soerensen and his company.

The marionette motif is undoubtedly very central in Dinesen's world.[7] To Dinesen life is a marionette comedy. This motif also illustrates the prevalence of the idea of the story in Dinesen's conception of life and art, for in her marionette comedies the story becomes more than a story. It becomes an archetypal story, a myth, the story created by God: "In the beginning was the story," says Cardinal Salviati. All of life becomes a great story in which we human beings have our own little story to enact to the best of our ability and knowledge. The characters who have faith in the story are rewarded with a sign or an image, discover their identity, and accept their destiny. Some of them are tragic figures, others are comic; but whether they are villains, victims, or fools does not seem to matter in the long run, for ultimately they are all marionettes and thus in the hands of God and the storyteller.

In the final analysis, the marionettes in Dinesen's world are performing in stories which illustrate two central themes in Dinesen's view of life: the theme of aristocratic pride and the theme of acceptance.

5

ARISTOCRACY

MANY CRITICS have commented on Dinesen's preference for the aristocrat and the virtues of aristocracy. She tends to surround herself in the tales with figures who have something of the *grand siècle* about them, figures for whom life is a noble and beautiful game to be played according to the rules of honor, and for whom pride is the highest virtue.

If we look at Dinesen's gallery of characters we find that it is primarily composed of high-ranking figures, often of noble birth. There are the kings: Christian VII and Erik. There are the princes: Prince Pozentiani, Prince Giovanni, Prince Gersdorff; the gentry: Calypso von Platen-Hallermund, Miss Malin Nat-og-Dag, Lady Flora Gordon, Baron von Brackel, Leopold von Galen, to mention only a few. There are the princes of the church: Cardinal Hamilcar von Sehestedt, Cardinal Salviati.

It should be made clear from the outset, however, that Dinesen's concept of aristocracy is not based on a class distinction. An aristocrat is one who has a particular view of life as well as a particular way of life. The best proof of this is that Dinesen's most succinct statement of the aristocratic attitude toward life occurs in a little essay called *Farah*, a brief account of the character of her Somali servant in Kenya.[1] Farah is here presented as the very embodiment of the aristocratic virtues.

Dinesen begins by calling Farah a gentleman and proceeds to define a gentleman as "a man who has the concepts of honor of his age and his milieu in his blood, and in whom they have become instinct, in the same manner as the rules of the game have become instinct with the true cricket or football player" (p. 11). In addition to this firmly embedded concept of honor, Farah has a passion for the grand gesture, the great repartee, and the heroic deed (p. 14). These aristocratic virtues of Farah and of the Somalis make her think of the heroes of the old Icelandic sagas. She thinks of Einar Tambaskaelver whose grand gesture and repartee at the battle of Svolder have outlived the knowledge of the result of the battle (p. 15). The ambition of these heroes was to be placed in the situation which would call for that great gesture which would forever make them immortal. Then Dinesen speaks of Farah's religion, the religion of Islam, a religion which ordains acceptance. The Mohammedan religion is an unconditional yes-saying to life, it affirms Allah and his will as it expresses itself in the world and in the destinies of men. The yes-saying of the Mohammedan is like that of Job: "God is great" (pp. 23-25). Farah is also without fear because he has a conviction that whatever happens is right, and he is without pity, she feels (pp. 28-29).

These are the basic virtues of the aristocrat then: a profound sense of honor; a great pride expressing itself in a passion for the grand gesture and the great repartee that will make one immortal; a yes-saying to life and to whatever fate may bring; and a lack of fear or pity.

One might speculate as to why Dinesen has made herself a spokesman for these rather "outmoded" virtues. Her background is undoubtedly an important factor.

Her grandfather and her father were aristocrats, heroic figures who sought glory in the field, excitement in the hunt, or power in statesmanship. Both won distinction in the field. So did her brother, Thomas Dinesen, who fought in the first World War with the Canadian forces. For his heroism in battle he was awarded the Victoria Cross, the only foreigner to be honored in this manner.[2]

Dinesen's twenty years in Africa must also have played a large role in the formation of her aristocratic outlook on life. There she lived in close contact with an eighteenth-century type of feudal culture, long since extinct in Europe.

Thus there is hardly any doubt that Dinesen's philosophy of life has been molded to a great extent by her family background and her own experience. She has, in person, experienced *l'ancien régime.* An important impetus toward the formation of her aristocratic view of life must have come from her father, whose conversations and writings have clearly made a great impression on her. Wilhelm Dinesen wrote a good deal, although only his *Jagtbreve* have become classic. He wrote about the uprising of the Commune in Paris, giving an eyewitness account of the happenings from the time of the proclamation of the Republic in September of 1870 to the fall of the Commune in May of 1871. He also wrote a number of essays, and travel books, and war memoirs.

Georg Brandes once wrote an essay about Wilhelm Dinesen in which he maintained that the central aspect of the latter's philosophy of life was "his disgust and contempt for the bourgeoisie as reigning power."[3] This contempt for the bourgeoisie, which Wilhelm's daughter has inherited, Brandes attributed to a family inheritance. Though not necessarily undemocratic in his political views, Dinesen based his contempt for the bourgeoisie on their sentimentality and lack of courage and pride. The bourgeoisie are always ready with their tears, he said, but "blood—that is, their own—with that they are not so generous."

Like his daughter he loved France and the French people. His point of view is French, said Brandes, and he thinks France is "the proudest, the noblest nation," and that Paris is "the capital of the world": "There is only one city, and that is Paris."

Dinesen's *Jagtbreve* are the reflections of a man who loves the life of the soldier, the hunter, and the poet because it is a life away from the worries of everyday existence.[4] The book consists primarily of reflections about hunting, fishing, wild animals, dogs, food, and wine. Many of these seem to be written by a person whose views and feelings are very similar to those of his daughter. They express a similar affirmation of a life of danger, courage, and pride. A few examples will illustrate this.

Dinesen defends the carnivorous birds on the basis that they force the smaller birds to become more intelligent: "How would it go, if there were no danger? Imagine, if the Lord said that for ten years not a ship would sink. Then we would become so courageous that we would sail in old newspapers. And sink during the eleventh."

Carnivorous birds he compares to royalty. He describes one as having a "regal carriage, a wild, proud, demanding, contemptuous glance": it does not "understand appreciation; it is without pity."

According to Brandes, Dinesen is intoxicated by "gunpowder-smoke" and "the lustre of bayonets": "In reality," says

Brandes, "he loves war for its own sake with the love of a soldier and an artist."[5] This is evident in his descriptions of war scenes, in which he shows a certain esthetic detachment. "The bayonet," he says,

> has like the diamond its *beaux jours;* there is a soul in both of them . . . it is not the diamond that lends glory to woman, it is the other way around; because it is not *das ewig Weibliche* that attracts the smile of the diamond and lights the fire in its interior, it is the young blood that charms both that and the bayonet and makes them shoot sparks.[6]

The tragic fate of the father must also have impressed itself upon the daughter's mind. Hunting, fishing, and writing did not give him what he longed for in life. As a landowner and farmer he must have longed, as so many of Dinesen's figures long, for the great and exciting life he had once enjoyed. His quiet existence was too narrow a world for his spirit, and in 1895 he took his own life. At this time his daughter was ten years old, but her basic philosophy of life must already have been formed, because it is so similar to her father's. It is similar in two fundamental respects: it is aristocratic in nature, and it praises a life of adventure and excitement, the sailors, vagabonds, soldiers, and poets of this world.

While Dinesen's own aristocratic background and her experiences in Africa have undoubtedly played a major role in the formation of her own conception of aristocracy, her reading must have provided an added impetus. The proud, noble, and fearless heroes of the old Icelandic sagas; the stoic soldiers of Alfred de Vigny with their faith in honor and nothing else; the fanatic aristocrats of Barbey d'Aurevilly: we meet them again in Dinesen's tales. Among modern writers it is more difficult to encounter heroes with a similar affirmation of life.[7] We have to turn back to the novels and tales of Joseph Conrad, a writer who has undoubtedly meant a great deal to Dinesen, in order to find a similar aristocratic view of life. Conrad, too, was interestingly enough a foreign aristocrat writing in English.

Like Dinesen, Conrad portrayed skeptics and melancholiacs who are finally, as Morton Dauwen Zabel puts it, "compelled out of isolation and personal illusion into the whole organism of life, into a 'solidarity with mankind.'"[8] It was Conrad who wrote: "Woe to the man whose heart has not learned while young to hope, to love—and to put its trust in life," but these words might as well have been written by Dinesen. The aristocrats in Dinesen's world, like the heroes in Conrad's novels, ultimately learn the lesson of Stein in *Lord Jim:* "The way is to the destructive element submit yourself, and with the exertions of your hands and feet in the water make the deep, deep sea keep you up."[9]

Like Joseph Conrad, Dinesen might be said to have produced in her tales "an elegiac memorial to a vanished and simpler order of life," to a world with other standards, those "of honor and fidelity."[10] Loyalty and fidelity to a code, the aristocratic code, is intimately bound up with the emphatic yes-saying to life which is one aspect of Dinesen's vision of life.

The image of life as a beautiful game in which the only requirement of the players is that they obey the rules of the game is first introduced in "The Old Chevalier." It is also a story which illustrates the idea of nemesis, a concept fundamentally related to the whole notion of aristocratic pride: the idea that life is dear, that one must pay the price of life.[11]

It is a story about Baron von Brackel and the dancer Nathalie as told to a young man by the Baron himself many years afterward. The story is told as an answer to the question "whether one is ever likely to get any real benefit, any lasting moral satisfaction, out of forsaking an inclination for the sake of principle" (SGT, p. 81).

Baron von Brackel relates how he sat one night on a bench in Paris when Nathalie suddenly appeared. Having just had a near brush with death (a young lady had tried to poison him), he is rather dejected. For this reason the appearance of Nathalie seems to him like a gift, a friendly act of fate. She follows him to his apartment, they sup and drink champagne, he undresses her, and they go to bed. After a few hours she gets up to leave and suddenly asks for twenty francs (as a certain Marie had told her to do, she says). The Baron gives her the twenty francs without any show of feeling, and she departs. Later he tries to find her again but is unable to do so.

To Nathalie the whole incident seems to be a gay adventure. There is an air of mystery about her; she acts as if she were keeping a secret. She is very innocent. To the Baron she is freedom, grace, and beauty personified.

Their relationship is one of utter freedom and security. The Baron has no thought of where she came from or where she is to go again, and he is not conscious of how she feels about him. He has no doubts or fears: that is, until some time during the night when he wakes up and thinks: "What am I to pay for this?" At this moment the distrust of the future appears, and it is then that Nathalie suddenly gets up and asks for twenty francs.

When she utters this request the Baron suddenly feels "as if all the illusions and arts with which we try to transform our world, coloring and music and dreams, had been drawn aside, and reality was shown to me, waste as a burnt house." This he realizes "was the end of the play," the moment in which she becomes "a human being, within an existence of her own," not just a gift to him (SGT, p. 102).

Her unexpected request places the Baron in a dilemma. His inclination is to keep her, but for the sake of principle he can not do this. "We two," he says, "had played. A rare jest had been offered me and I had accepted it; now it was up to me to keep the spirit of our game until the end. Her own demand was well within the spirit of the night." He realizes that he has the power to keep her "safe within the magic circle of her free and graceful and defiant spirit" simply by giving her the money, or to pass on to her "all the weight of the cold and real world" by hesitating to do so (SGT, p. 102).

As it happens he gives her the money, and he does so because her youth and her innocence call on the chivalrousness of his nature. And he defines chivalrousness as: "to love, or cherish, the pride of your partner, or of your adversary, as you will define it, as highly, or higher than, your own" (SGT, p. 103).

As a result of his fidelity to this code of chivalrousness the Baron loses Nathalie. He has observed the rules of the game: he has paid the price. He has accepted the jest in the spirit in which it was offered. By respecting the pride of his partner the Baron has made the relationship end as it began: within a magic circle of freedom, grace, and beauty. Fidelity to the code of chivalrousness is what gives order, balance, and style to human relations. In this sense life might be said to be like a game, a game of chess, in which the only demand of the players is that they abide by the rules. The aristocrat with his loyalty to these rules becomes, in fact, as Elling has pointed out, an esthetic type rather than a moral type: the laws governing human relations are like the laws of esthetics, the rules governing the composition of a fugue or a string quartet.[12] And the Baron undoubtedly benefited from his forsaking an inclination for the sake of principle (his "light-hearted dignity and self-reliance" attest to this), though he lost Nathalie (for fidelity to the code does not exclude tragedy or suffering).

There is another central theme in "The Old Chevalier," significant because it reveals the strong skepticism at the heart of Dinesen's vision of life. Two types of women are contrasted, and as a result of this contrast a significant statement is made about the nature of the aristocratic code.

The first is the emancipated woman, the woman who tried to poison the Baron. As an emancipated woman she is the rival of men, particularly her husband. She seeks to poison Baron von Brackel in a fit of jealousy because she has the feeling that he prefers her husband to her.

The second woman is Nathalie, who is presented as the representative of *das ewig Weibliche,* of woman as a symbol rather than an individual. Before von Brackel relates how he undressed Nathalie, he reflects about the difference between the "Woman" of his youth and the "women" of the present. He feels that emancipation is the destruction of the idea of woman, that it destroys the mystery and illusions that have been woven about her in the same manner as the clothes of today reveal rather than disguise the body (SGT, pp. 93-96).

In his day, says the Baron, a woman was like a work of art, "the product of centuries of civilization." A young girl was taught to shift "slowly the center of gravity of her being . . . from individuality to symbol." Women thought of themselves as guardians of a mystery, the mystery of the idea of woman. Women knew very well, of course, that there was no mystery. "I do not know," says the Baron,

> if you remember the tale of the girl who saved the ship under mutiny by sitting on the powder barrel with her lighted torch, threatening to put fire to it, and all the time knowing herself that it is empty. This has seemed to me a charming image of the woman of my time.

This image was so apt, he continues, because there they were, the women of his time, "keeping the world in order, and preserving the balance and rhythm of it, by sitting upon the mystery of life, and knowing themselves that there was no mystery" (SGT, pp. 94-96).

If looked upon as a central element in the whole story of von Brackel and Nathalie, the Baron's speech means this: Reality is deadly (the emancipated woman tried to kill von Brackel; a feeling of the cold, dead weight of reality descended on von Brackel when Nathalie asked him for twenty francs) and should not be unmasked. If you get too close to reality the illusion (which is all in the surface of things: clothes, manners, codes of behavior) is destroyed, and one thing is of no greater value than any other. Dreams, ideals, illusions, the fidelity to a code: all of these confer value on human life by disguising its essential and fundamental emptiness. They preserve the mystery which is no mystery. The aristocratic code is a tacit agreement among civilized individuals to preserve the beauty and grace of life by making it into an elegant game.

The most dramatic illustration of the aristocratic philosophy of life is found in "Sorrow Acre." This story, which is set in Denmark, seeks, in Milton's words, to justify the ways of God to man. It seeks to answer several related questions: Why is life so dear? Why is life so pitiless? Is there not a God who can temper the laws of necessity with mercy?

The central incident concerns a crime. Anne-Marie, a peasant woman, has a son who is accused and probably guilty of having set fire to a barn, and for this crime he is to be punished. When Anne-Marie pleads for her son the lord of the estate makes a stipulation: if she can mow a field of corn in one day, her son will be set free. Normally this is a task for three men. Anne-Marie succeeds, however, and the son is set free, but she dies from exhaustion.[13]

This incident, and particularly the role which the lord plays in it, is very shocking to his nephew, the young hero of the tale. Adam has been living in England and has been imbued with a number of the new liberal ideas: ideas about nature, justice, and the rights and freedoms of man; he even has some notions of going to the United States. To him the uncle, who has always been an embodiment of "law and order, the wisdom of life and kind guardianship," now appears as "a symbol of the tyranny and oppression of the world." At one point he tells the uncle to stop "this terrible thing," and he decides to leave the estate and go to the United States. Before evening, however, he has changed his mind. The reasons for this change are to be sought, I think, in his three conversations with the uncle, and in certain events which put the figure of the uncle in a new light (WT, pp. 34-36).

These conversations are central to the story. They concern the nature of comedy and tragedy. Adam has been reading a tragedy by the Danish poet Johannes Ewald (1743-81), entitled *Balder's Death* (1775), and at his suggestion the uncle also reads it during the course of the day.

During the first conversation Adam suggests "that we have not till now understood how much our Nordic mythology in moral greatness surpasses that of Greece and Rome." Adam feels that the gods of Greece and Rome were "mean, capricious and treacherous," while "the fair gods of Asgaard did possess the sublime human virtues; they were righteous, trustworthy, benevolent and even, within a barbaric age, chivalrous." The uncle disagrees with this statement: it was easier, he insists, for the Nordic gods to be virtuous because they were not as powerful as the gods of classical antiquity. The Nordic gods, he says, had at all times "by their side those darker powers which they named the Jotuns, and who worked the suffering, the disasters, the ruin of our world." The omnipotent Greek and Roman gods had "no such facilitation. With their omnipotence they take over the woe of the universe." Jove is superior to Odin because he "avowed his sovereignty, and accepted the world which he ruled" (WT, pp. 38-40).

The second conversation occurs after the uncle has read *Balder's Death*. This conversation concerns the nature of comedy and tragedy. Adam suggests that tragedy is, "in the scheme of life, a noble, a divine phenomenon." The uncle agrees that tragedy is a noble phenomenon, "but of the earth only, and never divine." "Tragedy," he says, "is the privilege of man, his highest privilege." As such it "should remain the right of human beings, subject, in their conditions or in their own nature, to the dire law of necessity. To them it is salvation and beatification." The gods, on the other hand, are not subject to necessity. As a result they can have no knowledge of the tragic: "When they are brought face to face with it they will, according to my experience, have the good taste and decorum to keep still, and not interfere."

"The true art of the gods is the comic," the uncle insists. "In the comic the gods see their own being reflected as in a mirror, and while the tragic poet is bound by strict laws, they will allow the comic artist a freedom as unlimited as their own." The comic artist may even mock at the gods.

On earth the aristocrats stand in lieu of the gods and have likewise emancipated themselves "from the tyranny of necessity." For this reason they must also "accept the comic with grace." And no master will "make a jest of his servants' necessity, or force the comic upon them." The aristocrat will not fear the comic: "Indeed," says the uncle, "the very same fatality, which, in striking the burgher or peasant, will become tragedy, with the aristocrat is exalted to the comic. By the grace and wit of our acceptance hereof our aristocracy is known" (WT, pp. 50-52).

The third conversation occurs after Adam has told the uncle to stop the terrible tragedy that is being enacted on the cornfield. The uncle answers that he is not at all forcing the old woman to go on. Adam's animadversions that the woman's death will come upon the uncle's head leave the uncle unperturbed. He says he has given Anne-Marie his word, and in his world the word is still the principle, the law of gravitation. Adam speaks for imagination, daring, and passion as greater powers of the word than those of any restricting or controlling law, but the uncle answers that it is impossible for him to stop Anne-Marie now without making light of her exploits, which would be making her into a comic figure. Adam's statement that he might go to the United States the uncle answers as follows: "Take service, there, with the power which will give you an easier bargain than this: That with your own life you may buy the life of your son" (WT, pp. 55-60).

The conversations between Adam and his uncle are evidently designed to illustrate the differences between two worlds: the world of the eighteenth century and the world of the postrevolutionary and romantic nineteenth century; between the feudal and aristocratic eighteenth century and the sentimental and humanitarian nineteenth century. The uncle represents a firm and well-defined order based on law, form, style, and continuity, and within this order his word is law. He has unlimited freedom within this order, but it is a freedom of the same kind as that possessed by the composer of a fugue or a symphony: it is circumscribed by certain rules. The uncle cannot break his word, and he must accept responsibility for the world he rules. Thus he is an aristocratic figure.

Adam, the rebel, cannot accept at first the inhumanity of

the uncle's forcing Anne-Marie to sacrifice her life for her son. At last he does so, however. Two things make him change his mind. He realizes that his uncle, too, is a tragic figure who has suffered as other human beings must suffer. The uncle has suffered because he has lost his only son. Thus the whole world that he represents is in danger of perishing, because it is based on the principle of continuance. Adam also comes to realize that the uncle is a comic figure, a representative here on earth of the comic-amoral divinities. He is a comic figure because, as a gypsy had prophesied, he will have a son produced for him by his wife and Adam (WT, p. 34). This is clearly indicated in the story. At the very outset it is suggested by the author that the real power in this aristocratic world is held by the women, because they alone can attest to the legitimacy of the sons who are to inherit the estates (WT, p. 32). When we are introduced to the wife of the uncle, she is standing naked in front of the mirror, admiring herself, while thoughts of a sexual nature flit through her mind: she thinks of the bulls and the stallions; she is conscious of an absence of some kind, and when a flea bites her she thinks it silly that only a flea should have the courage to risk its life "for her smoothness and sweet blood" (WT, pp. 43-45). In the afternoon she and Adam ride together in the field (WT, p. 47). Finally, it is said about Anne-Marie that to save her son is a sweet effort. This line also occurs in a popular tune, the words of which flit through the minds of both Adam and the wife: *"C'est un trop doux effort"* (WT, pp. 49-50). The sweet effort referred to in this connection, although obviously of another nature, is to the same end as that of Anne-Marie: to save a son.

Thus Adam is able to accept the feudal-aristocratic world, and his acceptance is based on a kind of religious experience: he realizes that all which lives must suffer, and that, consequently, there are no easy bargains in life. Adam realizes the unity of all things and accepts the world as it is. He also realizes that suffering brings greatness. By letting her play her role the uncle has conferred immortality on Anne-Marie: the field is forever after known as "Sorrow Acre." Adam learns to accept tragedy—not as a misfortune—but as a human privilege, because it confers on us ordinary human beings a greatness which is denied the gods and the aristocrats, denied those who are liberated from necessity.

One kind of tragedy is, however, not denied the aristocrats: the tragedy that springs from fidelity to the code of honor. A code of honor is a "luxury" which only aristocrats can afford. This is the motif of a story entitled "Copenhagen Season." It is set in 1870, a time when the world of aristocracy already had, as Dinesen puts it, "one foot in the grave" (LT, p. 254).

It is a story of the Ballegaard children, particularly Ib and Drude Angel. They are remarkable children in a number of ways. They possess three or four strong and unique qualities: "One of these was a great, wild happiness at being alive, what in French is called *la joie de vivre*. Each single thing included in daily human existence . . . called forth in them a rapture like that of a very young animal, the ecstasy of a foal let loose in a paddock." In addition, they were "almost ideally handsome and two of the sisters recognized beauties." "Each organ of their bodies was flawless," and "their five senses were as keen as those of wild animals" (LT, pp. 260-61).

The general feeling about "the brood of Ballegaard" was that "they were doomed, each of them in advance marked down for ruin." An old painter and sculptor with a great knowledge of the world forecasts their fate as follows: "This pretty litter of Ballegaard in the course of their lives will come to break most of our laws and commandments. But toward one law they will be unfailingly loyal: the law of tragedy. They have, each of them, it written in their heart" (LT, p. 263).

The theme of the story is developed around a conversation in one of the salons of Copenhagen. The conversation concerns progress. A lady maintains that "our great-grandchildren will have . . . many things," but they will have no hope of eliminating tragedy from life, because tragedy "is the outcome of the fall of man, and thus cannot possibly be easy to do away with." The painter disagrees with her. He insists that "tragedy will be an easy thing to do away with, as easy almost as the nose." People a hundred years from now will, he says, "be able to fly to the moon. But not one of them, to save his life, will be able to write a tragedy." He does not consider tragedy as the outcome of the fall of man, but as a

> . . . countermeasure taken by man against the sordid and dull conditions brought upon him by his fall. Flung from heavenly glory and enjoyment into necessity and routine, in one supreme effort of his humanity he created tragedy. How pleasantly surprised was not then the Lord. "This creature," He exclaimed, "was indeed worthy of being created. I have done well in making him, for he can make things for me which without him I cannot make" [LT, pp. 274-75].

Now, says the artist, what is that "absurd and preposterous thing, a ridiculous thing to carry about with you in life," which is "the most picturesque attribute of a human being," and "at the same time the rare spice by the aid of which tragedy is created?" The answer is honor, the idea of honor.[14] "All tragedies," he says,

> . . . are determined by the idea of honor. The idea of honor does not save humanity from suffering, but it enables it to write a tragedy. An age which can prove the wounds of the hero on the battlefield to be equally painful, whether in breast or in the back,

may produce great scientists and statisticians. But a tragedy it cannot write [LT, p. 276].

We need not recapitulate the following incidents which
are, of course, designed to illustrate the fact that the Ballegaard children are unfailingly loyal to the code of honor and
the law of tragedy. Ib Angel ultimately finds himself, after
the manner of classical tragedy, in a position in which he has
to choose between love and honor. He pays the price of life
and sacrifices love: "No, Adelaide, I would rather die" are
his last words.

Closely related to the concept of aristocratic pride and the
idea of nemesis is another concept, very fundamental in
Dinesen's philosophy of life: the concept of interdependence.
The motif of interdependence is central in several tales of
which "The Invincible Slaveowners" might serve as an in-
troductory example.

The tale concerns two sisters of aristocratic birth, Mizzi and
Marie, who now live in extreme poverty. Their pride forbids
them, however, to acknowledge this poverty to the world;
consequently they hide the fact that they are not able to keep
a servant by taking turns at playing the servant of each other.

Axel Leth, a young Danish nobleman staying at Baden-
Baden, becomes involved in the tragic tale. From the very
first moment he is impressed by the pride and majesty of
Mizzi, so obvious in her very walk: "She walked quickly, in
a defiant, disdainful gait, magnificently vital, as if at the same
time, and with all her might, giving and holding back herself
to the world" (WT, p. 130).

Mizzi seems to be so completely under the control of her
governess that it is impossible to approach her. This difficulty,

"and something pathetic in Mizzi's own figure, called upon the daring and chivalry of the courtiers. Each felt like Saint George with the dragon and the captive princess" (WT, p. 133).

Mizzi is utterly helpless without her governess. Axel reflects that "she must be dressed and undressed like a doll." Thus her "whole existence" is "based upon the constant, watchful, indefatigable labour of slaves" (WT, p. 136). Sadly he concludes that he will never be able to provide her with the necessities that her way of life requires.

Axel Leth is one of the melancholy young men in the world of Isak Dinesen. His encounter with the two sisters brings him an important realization, a new insight into life. He arrives at an understanding of interdependence, one of the basic concepts in Dinesen's *Weltanschauung*.

This insight comes to Axel as he takes the role of Frantz and acts as the servant of Mizzi. Standing in front of her— "with reverence, since he was now in livery"—he realizes that

> . . . the slave-owner's dependency upon the slave is strong as death and cruel as the grave. The slave holds his master's life in his hand, as he holds his umbrella. Axel Leth, with whom she was in love, might betray Mizzi; it would anger her, it might sadden her, but she was still, in her anger and melancholy, the same person. But her existence itself rested upon the loyalty of Frantz, her servant, and on his devotion, assent and support. His treachery would break the integrity of her being. If she were not, at any moment, sure that Frantz would die for her, she could not live [WT, p. 148].

After his return to Baden-Baden, Axel takes a walk to a little waterfall in the hills. There he sits thinking of Mizzi and of how very likely next year the parts will be interchanged: Lotti will be the slaveowner and Mizzi the slave.

What would become, he thought, of the two sisters, who had been so honest as to give life the lie, the partisans of an ideal, ever in flight from a blunt reality, the great, gentle ladies, who were incapable of living without slaves? For no slave, he reflected, could more desperately sigh and pine for his enfranchisement than they did sigh and pine for their slave, nor could freedom, to the slaves, ever be more essentially a condition of existence, the very breath of life than their slaves were to them [WT, pp. 150-51].

He finds a symbol for the condition of Mizzi and her sister in the waterfall. As the two sisters would go on playing their little game year by year, so

the clear stream, like a luminous column amongst the moss and the stones, held its noble outline unaltered through all the hours of day and night. In the midst of it there was a small projecting cascade, where the tumbling water struck a rock. That, too, stood out immutable, like a fresh crack in the marble of the cataract. If he returned in ten years, he would find it unchanged, in the same form, like a harmonious and immortal work of art [WT, p. 151].

And Axel wonders if there are similar phenomena in life: "Is there a corresponding, paradoxical mode of existing, a poised, classic, static flight and run?" He discovers one: "In music it exists, and there it is called a Fuga" (WT, p. 151).

In "The Invincible Slaveowners" the principle of interdependence is dramatized on the social level by the master-servant relationship. The symbol of the waterfall and the fugue seems to suggest, however, that the principle of interdependence has wider application. This becomes still more evident if we analyze some of the other tales based on this motif, and consider for a moment the two essays in which Dinesen has expressed her faith in the principle of interdependence (or interaction as she sometimes terms it): *Farah* and *En Baaltale*. The principle of interdependence is not only a social concept; it is a religious and artistic one as well.

In *Farah* Dinesen speaks of the pleasure we feel in being

part of a larger unity, but maintains that a genuine unity can only arise from dissimilar parts. A man and a woman form a true unity, not two men or two women. A hook and an eye likewise, but not two eyes. The world was created, according to the old Icelandic *Edda,* from hot *and* cold. This principle of the interaction of dissimilar parts is, however, most clearly illustrated by the master-servant relationship which is the topic of *Farah*.[15]

Farah was a true servant, and between him and Dinesen there existed an ideal master-servant relationship because they were so different. Between them were differences of sex, race, religion, milieu, and experience. Farah was indispensable to Dinesen in her dealings with the natives, and, as her economic position grew worse, he turned into a veritable magician when it came to providing the necessities of life. In a similar manner Farah's stature was enhanced through his association with his master. The relationship betwen the two of them can best be illustrated by a literary reference used by Dinesen. She speaks of some of the famous master-servant relationships in literature and thinks in particular of Don Quixote and Sancho Panza. The noble knight was highly dependent on his servant, but Sancho Panza would never have become immortal on his own: he needed a master to become himself.

In *En Baaltale* Dinesen speaks on a different topic: the relationship between the sexes. Again she refers to her "old faith in the importance of interaction and her conviction about the great riches and the unlimited possibilities that are contained in the correspondence and interplay of two dissimilar entities." [16] In this respect the relationship between man and woman is like the relationship between master and servant, and between the old and the young. Women should not try to imitate men, because that will destroy the true unity between them, a unity which has produced some of the finest

and noblest things in life: "Deeds, poetry, art, and taste."
Women should be, men should act (see p. 42).

In "The Consolatory Tale" the principle of interdependence
is seen at work in the problem of the relation between the
artist and his public. The writer Charlie Despard feels that
"all human relationships have in them something monstrous
and cruel. But the relation of the artist to the public is amongst
the most monstrous. Yes, it is as terrible as marriage" (WT,
p. 291). The monstrous nature of the relation of the artist
to his public is due, in Charlie's opinion, to the fact that "we
are, the artist and the public, much against our own will,
dependent upon one another for our very existence." By this
he does not mean an economic dependence: he means that

> . . . we are, each of us, awaiting the consent, or the co-operation
> of the other to be brought into existence at all. Where there is no
> work of art to look at, or to listen to, there can be no public either;
> that is clear, I suppose, even to you? And as to the work of art,
> now—does a painting exist at which no one looks?—does a book
> exist which is never read [WT, p. 292]?

So the public comes into being, and the relation between
the artist and his public is one without mercy on either side.
The artist and his work of art are at the mercy of the public
because only the public can, in Charlie Despard's opinion,
decide whether a work of art really exists or whether it is a
masterpiece or not. If the public denounces it as worthless,
it is worthless.

On the other hand, an artist behaves to his public "as the
Lord behaves to Job." "I know," says Charlie Despard,

> none so well, none so well as I, how the Lord needs Job as a pub-
> lic, and cannot do without him. Yes, it is even doubtful whether
> the Lord be not more dependent upon Job than Job upon the Lord.
> I have laid a wager with Satan about the soul of my reader. I have
> marred his path and turned terrors upon him, caused him to ride

on the wind and dissolved his substance, and when he waited for light there was darkness. And Job does not want to be the Lord's public any more than my public wishes to be so to me [WT, pp. 293-94].

There exists, then, a deep enmity between the artist and his public as between the Lord and Job. "Still," says Charlie, "in the end the two are reconciled; it is good to read about. For the Lord in the whirlwind pleads the defence of the artist, and of the artist only. He blows up the moral scruples and the moral sufferings of his public; he does not attempt to justify his show by any argument on right and wrong" (WT, p. 294). And Job turns out to be "the ideal public." Having listened to God's arguments, "he bows his head and foregoes his grievance; he sees that he is better off, and safer, in the hands of the artist than with any other power of the world, and he admits that he has uttered what he understood not."

After this initial discussion, Charlie's friend Aeneas tells him a consolatory tale. It develops the idea of interdependence a step further into a basic principle of all of life. The story is about the Persian Prince Nasrud-Din who likes to masquerade as a beggar and thus learn something "new as to the greatness and the power of Princes" (WT, p. 312). What he learns from the poor beggar Fath is, first, that "Life and Death are two locked caskets, each of which contains the key to the other" (WT, p. 303). Second, he learns that "man and woman are two locked caskets, of which each contains the key to the other" (WT, p. 309). Third, he learns from Fath that he and the beggar, "the rich and the poor of this world, are two locked caskets, of which each contains the key to the other" (WT, p. 312).

After listening to the story, Charlie leaves with this comment: "I shall go home now. I believe that I shall sleep tonight" (WT, p. 313). Though he does not really believe the tale to be a good one, he too has learned something about his condition as an artist, and how this condition is reflected in all aspects of life.

In "The Invincible Slaveowners" and in "A Consolatory Tale" the motif of interdependence is central. In a few other tales the motif is developed incidentally.

In "The Deluge at Norderney" Kasparson maintains that all things are sanctified by the play of the Lord "which is alone divine." The way in which he develops this argument suggests that he is speaking of the "divine" principle of interdependence. The subject is rather frivolous: Miss Nat-og-Dag's garter. Kasparson does not hesitate to draw far-reaching conclusions:

> If your garter be sanctified by my feeble old hand, so is my hand by your fine silk garter. The lion lies in wait for the antelope at the ford, and the antelope is sanctified by the lion, as is the lion by the antelope, for the play of the Lord is divine. Not the bishop, or the knight, or the powerful castle is sacred in itself, but the game of chess is a noble game, and therein the knight is sanctified by the bishop, as the bishop by the queen. Neither would it be an advantage if the bishop were ambitious to acquire the higher virtues of the queen, or the castle, those of the bishop. So we are sanctified when the hand of the Lord moves us to where he wants us to be. Here he may be about to play a fine game with us, and in that game I shall be sanctified by you, as you by any of us [SGT, pp. 14-15].

Later in the story Kasparson speaks of the fall of the divinity in heaven, which corresponds to the sorry state of monarchy on earth. God seems to have lost His feeling for greatness, and King Louis Philippe is a failure because he is trying to be just like a plain ordinary citizen. "And the good God," says Kasparson, "whom Louis Philippe and his bourgeoisie worship today, he has all the virtues of a righteous human being; he claims no divine privileges except by virtue of his virtues. We, we no more expected a moral attitude in our God than we meant to hold our great King responsible to the penal law." Kasparson, abhorring this "humane God," feels again a longing for the time when "in the nights of Mexico, I felt the great traditions rise up again of a God who did not give a pin for our commandments" (SGT, p. 58).

Thus there is no longer any place for the aristocrats on earth or in heaven. Having not been "brought up to a reasonable content," as Kasparson puts it, but having been brought up to be charlatans, they will "cut a finer figure in hell." They find themselves in the position of the well-trained bull in the bullring were the King suddenly to decide to stop the fight in order to avoid bloodshed. The "plebeian bull" would undoubtedly be thankful for this compassionate decision. But "what would the true fighting bull think of it? He might go for the audience, even for the master of ceremonies then." He has been bred and reared to fight: to stop the fight is to deprive him of his reason for being. This is the world in which the basic principle of interdependence is lost.

Interdependence is one of the basic concepts in Dinesen's philosophy of life. As such it by no means offers a solution to the problems of life: rather it simply invites its own acceptance as the only real and genuine principle of order in human existence. Isak Dinesen, says Jørgen Gustava Brandt, does not seek "a compromise or solution for the sufferings and troubles of this world, but to find the great *balance* in all relations, that *tension* which one might call the symposion of existence, an art of life which is related to the ropedancer's or to that of the Ecclesiastes." [17]

6

THE
ART OF
ACCEPTANCE

I N HIS conversations with Aeneas, Charlie Despard referred to the Book of Job when he spoke of the relation between the artist and his public. This was no mere coincidence. The Book of Job is a central document of the Bible as far as Isak Dinesen is concerned. The numerous references to this book scattered throughout the tales attest to this fact.

Ernst Frandsen notes that the Book of Job is Dinesen's "sacred book," because the theme of her work is acceptance.[1] He also remarks that God seems to defend Himself against Job on artistic grounds, and for this reason God stands in the same relation to Job as the artist to his public.

Jørgen Gustava Brandt also comments on the significance of the Book of Job for all of Dinesen's writings. This, he says, is because Isak Dinesen is not an artist of rebellion like so many contemporary writers, but an artist of acceptance and affirmation. To Brandt, Dinesen is "the author of the great reconciliation, the reconciliation to the world, to life, to existence, to God, reconciliation by means of complete submission, the most consistently voluntary openness to be found in the European literature of this century, the proudest form of submission." [2] And Brandt calls this "the greatest motif" in Dinesen's works.

We need only compare Isak Dinesen to some contemporary European and American authors to recognize, as Brandt does, her uniqueness in this respect. Thomas Mann in his late works achieved a similar type of affirmation. But Pär Lagerkvist and Albert Camus are authors of rebellion, not so much against society as were the writers of the 1930's, but against life, against God, against the injustice inherent in human existence. They are, in the words of Albert Camus, "metaphysical rebels." [3]

Dinesen's attitude to life, says Brandt, is founded on "the highest degree of consciousness and openness, an unconditional yes-saying to all of existence, which embraces all that we can experience, and which like Job completely surrenders to the conditions." [4]

Brandt compares Dinesen to those in our time "who live on the defensive," and "who want to make themselves secure in all respects against life and the world about us." Dinesen, he says, is "willing to pay the price of life," and for that reason she enjoins acceptance as a way, "a new possible way of living in complete freedom." As such Dinesen's way is not a solution to the problems of life, he insists, for "like all great prophets she provides no solution," just the way to freedom through acceptance.

Most of Dinesen's tales do reflect a rather grim view of human existence. Our fondest expectations come to nought. To strive for social justice is folly. Our manners, our ideals, our dreams are only veils of illusion making life bearable because they mask the essential nothingness of existence. If we get too close to reality one thing is no more valuable than the other. Before God, life is a joke, and God Himself is amoral. You can never be sure whether you are in the service of God or the Devil. There are no easy solutions to any human problems: Nemesis rules and requires us to pay the price of life, which is high. There is no reason for moral indignation since there are no villains in this world, only fools.

There is only one way to freedom: acceptance of life, of the world, of God. The splendid and irresistible aristocrats who have courage, imagination, and pride accept their destiny and are set free, unlike the melancholiacs or the bourgeoisie who merely observe life without living it, or lose life by trying to guard themselves against its dangers.

Brandt also points to the fact that Dinesen does not accept the doctrine of salvation contained in the New Testament. The Old Testament is her sacred book, and her God is an Old Testament God.[5] There are many references to Christ in the tales, but He is very often represented as a comic figure, or as a man whose message is unacceptable.

Christ is a comic figure because He is a god, and thus not subject to "the dire laws of necessity." This idea is expressed in "Sorrow Acre." "Tragedy is the privilege of man, his highest privilege," says the uncle. For this reason,

> the God of the Christian Church Himself, when He wished to ex-
> perience tragedy, had to assume human form. And even at that the
> tragedy was not wholly valid, as it would have become had the
> hero of it been, in very truth, a man. The divinity of Christ con-
> veyed to it a divine note, the moment of comedy. The real tragic
> part, by the nature of things, fell to the executors, not to the vic-
> tim [WT, pp. 50-51].

In "The Deluge at Norderney" Miss Nat-og-Dag, who refers to Christ as the "conscientious young male of the Gospel," argues that God has a penchant for masquerades because He seems to her "to have been masquerading pretty freely at the time when he took on flesh and dwelt amongst us. Indeed, had I been hostess of the wedding at Cana, I might have resented the feat a little" (SGT, pp. 18, 24).

In "The Fish" Christ's philosophy is represented as being unacceptable to kings or aristocrats: it is said to be a philosophy for carpenters and fishermen (WT, pp. 236-37).

Lady Flora Gordon in "The Cardinal's Third Tale" repudiates Christ. When Father Jacopo tells her: "You doubt . . . that we be all one!—and yet you are aware that one is dead for us all!"; her answer is: "Not for me. . . . I beg to be excused! Never in my life have I asked any human being—much less any god—to die for me, and I must insist that my own personal account be kept altogether outside this statement" (LT, pp. 86-87).

If Christ is a comic figure with a rather unacceptable message of salvation and redemption, God is a great artist. In "A Consolatory Tale" we have seen God represented as standing in the same relation to Job as the artist does to his public. God does not attempt to justify Himself to Job by any argument of right and wrong; His defense is the whirlwind. In other words, the Lord impresses Job with His power: "Wilt thou disannul my judgment?" He asks. "Knowest thou the ordinances of heaven? Hast thou walked in the search of the depth? Canst thou lift up thy voice to the clouds? Canst thou bind the sweet influence of the Pleiades?" Before such questions Job bows his head and forgoes his grievance: "he sees that he is better off, and safer, in the hands of the artist than with any other power of the world, and he admits that he has uttered what he understood not" (WT, p. 294).

In "The Young Man with the Carnation" the Lord also tries to impress Charlie with His power:

"Who made the ships, Charlie?" he asked. "Nay, I know not," said Charlie, "did you make them?" "Yes," said the Lord, "I made the ships on their keels, and all floating things. The moon that sails in the sky, the orbs that swing in the universe, the tides, the generations, the fashions. You make me laugh, for I have given you all the world to sail and float in, and you have run aground here, in a room of the Queen's Hotel to seek a quarrel" [WT, p. 25].

God is also like the artist in that He has the greatest imagination. When Charlie looks back on the happenings of the night before, "with the experienced eye of an author of fiction, they moved him as mightily as if they had been out of one of his own books. 'Almighty God,' he said from the bottom of his heart, 'as the heavens are higher than the earth, so are thy short stories higher than our short stories'" (WT, p. 23).

In "The Roads Round Pisa" God is again represented as the all-powerful artist with a great range of the imagination. "Humanity," says the poet Monti,

the men and women on this earth, are only the plaster of God, and we, the artists, are his tools, and when the statue is finished in marble or bronze, he breaks us all up. When you die you will probably go out like a candle, with nothing left, but in the mansions of eternity will walk Orlando, the Misanthrope and my Donna Elvira. Such is God's plan of work, and if we find it somehow slow, who are we that we should criticize him, seeing that we know nothing whatever of time or eternity [SGT, p. 188]?

The figures in "The Roads Round Pisa" are marionettes who are trying to break up the statues that God is fashioning before they are finished. For this reason God has to stage a great intrigue comedy in order to punish them, and show them that His imagination is greater than man's: "Always," says Prince Pozentiani, "we fail because we are too small. I grudged the boy Mario that, in a petty grudge. And in my vanity I thought that I should prefer an heir to my name, if it was to be, out of a ducal house. Too small I have been, too small for the ways of God" (SGT, p. 207). The old Countess says: "Life is a mosaic work of the Lord's, which he keeps filling in bit by bit. If I had seen this little bit of bright color as the centerpiece, I would have understood the pattern, and would not have shaken it all to pieces so many times, and given the good Lord so much trouble in putting it together again" (SGT, p. 215).

In "The Deluge at Norderney" Kasparson praises God's great imagination as it manifested itself in the creation of the world. Speaking in particular of the matters of love and marriage, he says:

> Every human being has, I believe, at times given room to the idea of creating a world himself. The Pope, in a flattering way, encouraged these thoughts in me when I was a young man. I reflected then that I might, had I been given omnipotence and a free hand, have made a fine world. I might have bethought me of the trees and rivers, of the different keys in music, of friendship and innocence; but upon my word and honor, I should not have dared to arrange these matters of love and marriage as they are, and my world should have lost sadly thereby. What an overwhelming lesson to all artists! Be not afraid of absurdity; do not shrink from the fantastic. Within a dilemma, choose the most unheard-of, the most dangerous, solution. Be brave, be brave [SGT, pp. 54-55]!

When God impresses the artist or Job with the fact that He created the world, He does not argue that this world is "the best of all possible worlds," only that it is "sublime." This is made clear in the conversation between the Lord and His servant, the artist-priest, as told by Cardinal Salviati in "The Cardinal's First Tale." "You are aware," God says, "that I am almighty. And you have before you the world which I have created. Now give me your opinion on it. Do you take it that I have meant to create a peaceful world?" The candidate answers in the negative. "Or that I have," continues the Lord, "meant to create a pretty and neat world?" Again a negative answer. "Or a world easy to live in?" the Lord asks. "O good Lord, no!" answers the candidate. "Or do you," the Lord finally asks, "hold and believe that I have resolved to create a sublime world, with all things necessary to the purpose in it, and none left out?" When the young man gives an affirmative answer, he is accepted (LT, pp. 21-22).[6]

But God has other attributes. In "The Deluge at Norderney" He is said to have a penchant for masquerades, a quality which is also stressed by Mira Jama in "The Dreamers." He says: "I have been trying for a long time to understand God. Now I have made friends with him. To love him truly you must love change, and you must love a joke, these being the true inclinations of his own heart" (SGT, p. 355). Mira Jama's statement should be qualified, however, by Pellegrina Leoni's in "Echoes." She says to the sailor Niccolo:

> Yet I can tell you that the Lord likes a jest, and that a *da capo*—which means: taking the same thing over again—is a favorite jest of his. He may have wanted, now, a sailor stuck on the top of a mountain, such as was Noah, whose name begins with the same letter as yours [LT, p. 160].

Pellegrina's statement about God's love of repetition recalls our earlier discussion of marionette and myth: how God occasionally runs out of patterns and has to repeat some of the more satisfactory ones over and over again.

Pellegrina makes another interesting observation about God in her conversation with Niccolo. They are speaking of Christ, and Pellegrina says:

> I, too, have heard of Him. He will have been pleasant to talk with, for He was highly urbane, and said things to people which they must have been happy to hear. He said: "Be ye therefore perfect!" And I tell you, Niccolo, there is not a singer in the whole world

who is not longing to hear those words spoken. Yet He went through much, even more than we. For He will, in His quality of God, have known man's dreadful obstinacy, which may well be incomprehensible to a God. And He will also, in His quality of man, have known God's terrifying fancifulness, incomprehensible to man [LT, p. 165].

The important statements here refer to "man's dreadful obstinacy" and "God's terrifying fancifulness, incomprehensible to man." So many of Dinesen's heroes and heroines are dreadfully obstinate. They struggle against their own destiny, they kick against the pricks, they try to break up God's pattern or plan, they try to set things right according to their own limited imagination or knowledge. And they have to undergo traumatic experiences in order to attain an acceptance of God's will and His "incomprehensible fancifulness." However, no matter how obstinate they may be, and no matter how much they fight against their destiny, they almost all attain this final acceptance.

As I have already mentioned, most of the tales are woven in such a manner that the action in them, or the tales told within them, provide the central figure with a recognition of his own identity and an insight into the real nature of life, an experience which brings him to an acceptance of himself, his own role in life, and of God and the world. Prince Pozentiani, Lady Carlotta, Charlie Despard, Adam, Emilie Vandamm, and Lady Flora Gordon: all are rebels and dreadfully obstinate, but they all arrive at a kind of reconciliation with the world and an acceptance of the nature of things. Sometimes this reconciliation and acceptance is based on a tragic recognition: Adam, Ib Angel, Baron von Brackel, and Axel Leth have this experience. The tragic recognition is, of course, attained particularly by characters in the tales based on the motif of aristocratic pride. Sometimes the experience is based on a comic perception: the characters recognize that they have been fools in God's great comedy. We have already encountered this comic perception in the tales centering around the marionette motif. It is also found in two other tales which are not based on this motif: "The Young Man with the Carnation" and "The Cardinal's Third Tale." The first of these I have already discussed in this context.

"The Cardinal's Third Tale" is the story of Lady Flora Gordon, a Scots noblewoman of a somewhat unusual size. When the story begins she is visiting Rome, a city to which she has gone "in order to confirm by personal observation her deep distrust of all that its name implies" (LT, p. 65). This is a habit of hers: "I felt," says Cardinal Salviati, "that she had, wherever she had traveled, inspected the loveliest and most famous countries and cities of our poor earth with this same purpose: to corroborate her essential suspicion of both Creator and creation" (LT, p. 66). She is, not surprisingly, a great admirer of the works of Jonathan Swift.

Father Jacopo, a humble Roman priest, and Lady Flora Gordon become good friends and discuss matters of religion and theology during their meetings. Lady Flora proves herself to be an able debater. Father Jacopo tries to tell her of the perfection of the universe and of the oneness of all things, of all creation. Most eloquently Father Jacopo speaks of the likeness of all things, because this likeness is, he says, "proof that all things of this world are issued from one and the same workshop; it is in each thing the authentic signature of the Almighty." He continues in the same vein:

> In this sense of the word, Milady, likeness is love. For we love that to which we bear likeness, and we will become like that to which we love. Therefore, the beings of this world who decline to be like anything will efface the divine signature and so work out their own annihilation. In this way did God prove His love of mankind: that

He let Himself be made in the likeness of man. For this reason it is wise and pious to call attention to likenesses, and Scripture itself will speak in parables, which means comparisons [LT, p. 85].

The subject of likenesses leads Lady Flora to think of the "pretty comparisons" in the Song of Songs, particularly of the comparison of the bride to "a rose of Sharon," and of her belly to "a heap of wheat." To Father Jacopo these are significant likenesses. "Does not the rose," he asks, "clearly exhibit to our eyes the signature of the workshop from which she is issued? And does not the heap of wheat, too, exhibit it?" And he quotes a few lines from the Song of Songs:

Set me as a seal upon thine heart, as a seal upon thine arm, for love is strong as death; jealousy is cruel as the grave. Many waters cannot quench love, neither can the floods drown it: if a man would give all the substance of his house for love . . . it would utterly be contemned [LT, p. 86].

These arguments are, however, unacceptable to the arrogant Lady Flora, and Father Jacopo is near despair. He feels, however, that there is one hope left for her: her challenge of heaven is so great that it cannot go unanswered by the heavenly powers.

Feeling that one of Lady Flora's problems is that she has never encountered an equal opponent, Father Jacopo brings her to Saint Peter's, a church which impresses her deeply, particularly because of its size.

The end of the story relates of the manner in which Lady Flora met her destiny. Cardinal Salviati tells of his meeting with her at a resort in Ascoli some time after she left Rome. He found her still as witty as ever, but the Cardinal notices that a touch of "gentle and delicate irony" had been added. In addition, there was "a new joviality, a mirthful forbearance with and benevolence toward the frailty of humanity" about her person, even when the topic of a conversation would turn to events of an amorous nature (LT, p. 96).

One evening she tells the Cardinal what happened to her. The evening before leaving Rome she went to the cathedral and stood contemplating the figure of St. Peter. While she stood in front of the statue, it seemed to her as if the face of the Apostle changed, "and as if his lips moved faintly." Then a young man of the people entered and kissed the foot of the statue. Not knowing what drove her to follow his example, Lady Flora stepped forward and kissed St. Peter's foot on the same spot, and, she says, "like him I held my lips against it for a long time." The result: "Four weeks later, as I was staying in Missolonghi, by the Bay of Patras, I discovered the sore on my lip. My English doctor, who accompanied me, at once diagnosed the disease and named it to me. I was not ignorant, I knew the name." Then she adds: "I stood, your Eminence, before the glass and looked at my mouth. Then I bethought myself of Father Jacopo. To what, I thought, does this bear a likeness? To a rose? Or to a seal?" (LT, p. 98).

Thus Lady Flora's challenge of heaven did not go unanswered. God responded, and he responded in a manner consonant with his "incomprehensible fancifulness," for the seal he set upon her heart was a strange one indeed. However, even though the sign she received may appear as a bad joke, the effect of it was miraculous, for by this miracle Lady Flora was, as Børge G. Madsen puts it, "redeemed of her isolation and brought closer to the people." [7] The truth of Father Jacopo's words about the perfection of the universe and of the oneness of all creation had finally been revealed to her, but not until she had forced God to stage a little comedy calling her attention to likenesses.

Tales such as "The Roads Round Pisa," "The Young Man

with the Carnation," and "The Cardinal's Third Tale" are not only superb examples of Dinesen's storytelling at its best; they also serve quite well to illustrate two points previously made in regard to Dinesen's art of fiction: that what matters, first and foremost, is the story (for the characters in these tales do not matter: they are marionettes); and that the plot is designed to bring the characters to a point of higher awareness.

These tales have, in addition, another and still more significant feature in common. The insight which these characters obtain is a comic perception: they come to realize that they have been fools in God's great marionette comedy. They recognize how limited their imagination is compared to God's. In Dinesen's world God is the greatest artist because He has the greatest imagination. When her characters, a Charlie Despard, a Flora Gordon, recognize their limitations and affirm the power of God they affirm the artist and the story, for God is the greatest storyteller of them all: "In the beginning was the story." What the characters realize is that they have been bad marionettes: they have not had faith in the story, the story of life. Like the King in the *Arabian Nights* they learn of the solidarity of mankind and acquire a love of life. And they do so through the story. Thus when Dinesen vindicates God to man, as God vindicated Himself to Job, she vindicates the art of romance and the free play of the imagination: she vindicates the story. This is her greatest theme, but at this point it has become so closely interwoven with the theme of acceptance that the two are one and indistinguishable from each other.

7

AFRICA

All sorrows can be borne if you put them into a story or tell a story about them.

A T A FIRST GLANCE *Out of Africa* appears very different from the tales.[1] It is an autobiographical work, and it is descriptive in nature. Yet it is possible to demonstrate, I think, a deep affinity between *Out of Africa* and the rest of Dinesen's writing. The Africa that we meet in this volume is, in fact, the visible correspondent of Dinesen's fictional world. This explains why Harald Nielsen is not pleased with Dinesen's picture of Africa. He feels it to be lacking in concreteness and vividness: it suffers, he maintains, from the fact that there is too much of Dinesen's art and personality associated with it. What Nielsen does not realize is that Dinesen's Africa is primarily a construct, a world that bears the trademark of its maker.[2]

Harald Nielsen would probably prefer to read what Richard Wright or John Gunther has written about Africa in recent years, for in their books he would find a picture of Africa as it is today. Dinesen writes about a different Africa, an Africa that is rapidly disappearing.

She realizes that Africa is "changing and has already changed since I lived there," and for this reason she feels that her writings "may have a sort of historical interest" (OA, p. 21). As in her tales Dinesen is describing a world and a way of life that has disappeared or is in the process of disappearing.

Dinesen has always been an admirer of the eighteenth century, and in Africa she met the eighteenth century in reality: "Life out there was, I believe, rather like 18th century England: one might often be hard up for cash, but life was still rich in many ways, with the lovely landscape, dozens of horses and dogs and a multitude of servants."[3] The Africa Dinesen writes about is a preindustrial, prerevolutionary civilization, feudal in structure, and for this reason very much like the European civilization which she recreates in the tales. And there, in Africa, Dinesen ruled like an eighteenth-century feudal lord over a coffee plantation of some six thousand acres, with squatters holding a few acres each in return for a few days of work each year on the plantation proper.

Dinesen's Africa is, like the world of the tales, an esthetic construct, a beautiful, well-organized, formal world. The landscape, the animals, the people, the events on the farm: all these are fitted into a world of such formal perfection that it appears as a tapestry.

The tone is set already on the first pages of the book. The geographical position and the height of the land (over six thousand feet), says Dinesen, combined to create "a landscape that had not its like in all the world" (OA, p. 3). Here Africa was "distilled up through six thousand feet, like the strong and refined essence of a continent." The colors of the landscape were "dry and burnt, like the colors in pottery." The trees had a foliage different from that of the trees in Europe, growing not "in bows or cupolas, but in horizontal layers, and the formation gave to the tall solitary trees a likeness to the palms, or a heroic and romantic air like fullrigged ships with their sails clewed up." The views were "immensely wide," and as a result "everything that you saw made for greatness and freedom, and unequalled nobility" (OA, p. 4). The "chief feature of the landscape," says Dinesen, "was the air":

> In the middle of the day the air was alive over the land, like a flame burning; it scintillated, waved and shone like running water, mirrored and doubled all objects, and created great Fata Morgana. Up in this high air you breathed easily, drawing in a vital assurance and lightness of heart.

The distant mountain of Ngong was "crowned with four noble peaks," and the clouds traveling with the wind toward the summit were majestic: "Many times I have from my house followed these mighty processions advancing, and have wondered to see their proud floating masses, as soon as they had got over the hills, vanish in the blue air and be gone" (OA, p. 5). The hill country was "tremendously big, picturesque and mysterious," and here the buffalo, the eland, and the rhino roamed. Along the very ridge of the hills was a game path: "One morning, at the time that I was camped in the hills, I came up here and walked along the path, and I found on it fresh tracks and dung of a herd of Eland. The big peaceful animals must have been up on the ridge at sunrise, walking in a long row, and you cannot imagine that they had come for any other reason than just to look, deep down on both sides, at the land below" (OA, pp. 6-7).

There are familiar features in this style. We recognize the generous use of metaphors and similes, the note of artifice, the preference for the picturesque, and the use of rhetoric to create a feeling of nobility, greatness, and pride.

As in the tales Dinesen transforms reality into artifice through a liberal use of metaphors and similes. As far as the rendering of the landscape is concerned, we have already encountered some of these: the descriptions of the landscape, the trees, and the distant mountain of Ngong (see pp. 127-28). There are many others. Speaking of the "mysterious region" of the African forest, Dinesen writes: "You ride into the depths of an old tapestry, in places faded and in others darkened with age, but marvellously rich in green shades" (OA, p. 64). Flying over the plains, she observes that the whole landscape "looked like delicately marked tortoise-shell" and the lake lay there "in the bleak tawny land like a big bright aquamarine" (OA, p. 239). Describing the activities on the coffee plantation, Dinesen relates of the times when the coffee would be dry and ready to take out of the dryer during the night:

> That was a picturesque moment, with many hurricane lamps in the huge dark room of the factory, that was hung everywhere with cobwebs and coffeehusks, and with eager glowing dark faces, in the light of the lamps, round the dryer; the factory, you felt, hung in the great African night like a bright jewel in an Ethiope's ear [OA, p. 8].

Most of the metaphors and similes that serve to transform reality into artifice are, however, to be found in connection with the description of animals and people.

Seeing a herd of elephants "travelling through dense Native forest, where the sunlight is strewn down between the thick creepers in small spots and patches," Dinesen says the scene was, "in giant size, the border of a very old, infinitely precious Persian carpet, in the dyes of green, yellow and black-brown" (OA, p. 15). Turning a corner in the forest, "we saw a leopard sitting on the road, a tapestry animal" (OA, p. 65). Watching the progression of giraffes across the plain, Dinesen thinks of them "in their queer, inimitable, vegetative gracefulness, as if it were not a herd of animals but a family of rare, long-stemmed, speckled gigantic flowers slowly advancing" (OA, p. 15). The various kinds of gazelles that come to the green places to graze "look like toy animals stood upon a billiard table," and the eland "seem to have come out of an old Egyptian epitaph" (OA, p. 99). Flying low over a lake and suddenly descending, Dinesen and Denys saw thousands of flamingoes which at their approach "spread out in large circles and fans, like the rays of a setting sun, like an artful Chinese pattern on silk or porcelain, forming itself and changing, as we looked at it" (OA, p. 239). On a narrow path in the forest Dinesen also met the giant forest hog, "a rare person to meet. He came suddenly past me, with his wife and three young pigs, at a great speed, the whole family looking like uniform, bigger and smaller figures cut out in dark paper, against the sunlit green behind them" (OA, pp. 65-66). Lulu, the pet antelope, had "all the air of a young Chinese lady of the old school with laced feet," and "it was a rare thing to hold such a perfect thing in your hands" (OA, p. 68). She was "unbelievably beautiful" and looked "like a minutely painted illustration to Heine's song of the wise and gentle gazelles by the flow of the river Ganges" (OA, p. 71).

Even the people, the natives, become part of this artificial, tapestry world. The black matron of the native hospital loved to put on paint and powder so thick that "within her white coiffe her broad face looked like the face of those Russian wooden dolls which will unscrew, and have then got another doll inside them, and another inside that, and which are sold under the name of Katinka" (OA, p. 125). The young Masai warrior Kabero is described as having "the general rigid, passive, and insolent bearing of the Moran, that makes of him an object for contemplation, such as a statue is, a figure which is to be seen, but which itself does not see" (OA, p. 135). The faces of the Masai "with the high cheek-bones and boldly swung jaw-bones, are sleek, without a line or groove in them, swollen: the dim unseeing eyes lie therein like two dark stones tightly fitted into a mosaic; altogether the young Morani have a likeness to mosaics" (OA, p. 135). The native girls on the farm sit at the festival "as quiet as glass-eyed dolls of dark wood," smoking their little cigars (OA, p. 159). The Kikuyu rub themselves with a kind of red chalk in which "the young people themselves look fossilized, like statues cut in rock" (OA, p. 159). The girls cover their leather garments and themselves with the earth, "and look all one with them,—clothed statues in which the folds and draperies are daintily carried out by a skilled artist." Kamante, her servant, makes Dinesen think of a gargoyle: "with a very slight alteration, he might have sat and stared down, on the top of the cathedral of Notre Dame in Paris" (OA, p. 32). Intense and bright and lively of nature, he would, she says, "in a painting have made a spot of unusually intense coloring" (OA, p. 32).

Some of the images not only suggest the qualities of artifice and tapestry, but evoke a world of animals and objects that is self-contained and complete within itself. There is the herd of eland, "big peaceful animals . . . walking in a long row" along the path of the ridge; "you cannot imagine that they had come for any other reason than just to look, deep down on both sides, at the land below" (OA, pp. 6-7). There is the herd of buffalo, 129 animals in all, "come out of the morning mist under a copper-sky, one by one, as if the dark and massive, ironlike animals with the mighty horizontally swung horns were not approaching, but were being created before my eyes and sent out as they were finished" (OA, p. 15). There is the herd of elephants traveling through the dense forests, "pacing along as if they had an appointment at the end of the world" (OA, p. 15). The sight of the giant forest hog and his family was "a glorious sight, like a reflection in a forest pool, like a thing that had happened a thousand years ago" (OA, p. 66). Lulu, the pet antelope, is described as "a superior, independent being," "a young princess in exile" who has come into "her full queenly estate" (OA, p. 74). She stands "quietly on her divine rights"; gazing at Dinesen, she does not wink, and her eyes are without expression. "I remembered," says Dinesen, "that the Gods or Goddesses never wink, and felt that I was face to face with the ox-eyed Hera" (OA, p. 75). Finally, there are the oxen: "They have moist, limpid, violet eyes, soft muzzles, silky ears, they are patient and dull in all their ways; sometimes they look as if they were thinking about things" (OA, p. 263).

With such means Dinesen achieves an effect similar to that of the tales. She creates an artificial, stylized world, stamped with her own imagination, in which people, animals, and things are like works of art, self-contained, noble, and proud.[4]

There is another important feature characteristic of both the tales and *Out of Africa*. That is the tendency to make events and actions into drama or ritual, into ballet or opera, into myth. The open-air dance at the farm is compared to "those old pictures of a battle, observed from an eminence, in which you will see the cavalry advancing at one side, while the artillery takes up its position at the other, and isolated figures of ordnance officers gallop diagonally across the field of view" (OA, p. 160). While the Somali girls learn to knit, they laugh "as over a comical puppet-show" (OA, p. 179). The long procession of cattle "sedately marching along the narrow bank looked against the sky like Noah's procession of animals going into the Ark; and Old Knudsen himself, counting them, his stick under his arm, looked like the boat-builder Noah, content in the thought that everybody but himself was soon to drown" (OA, p. 192). Charcoal-burning in the African forest becomes a "mise-en-scène," because the place "had a theatrical atmosphere":

. . . the dark kilns themselves looked like tents on the stage: the place was a smugglers' or soldiers' camp in a romantic Opera. . . . In the surroundings, the small crooked form of Old Knudsen fitted in wonderfully well, flickering about, red-topped, agile, now that he had got a favorite job to attend to, sneering and encouraging, like a Puck grown old and blind and very malicious [OA, pp. 188-89].

While Dinesen and Denys hunt lions at night the lighted torch in the forest changes the whole world "into a brilliantly lighted stage," and the whole hunt takes on the quality of a classical tragedy (OA, p. 235). The lion, as it sits on the carcass of a giraffe, makes her think of a line from a poem: "Lion Passant Or" (OA, p. 230). After she has shot the lion, she walks around the carcass of the giraffe and thinks: "There it was,—the fifth act of a classic tragedy. They were all dead now. . . . The lioness, lying on her back, had a great haughty snarl on her face, she was the femme fatale of the tragedy" (OA, pp. 230-31).

As in the tales, literary references are abundant. Speaking of the books she was reading while in Africa, Dinesen says: "All Walter Scott's characters were at home in the country and might be met anywhere; so were Odysseus and his men, and strangely enough many figures from Racine. Peter Schlemihl had walked over the hills in seven-league boots, Clown Agheb the honey-bee lived in my garden by the river" (OA, pp. 363-64). In the same manner the figures and the landscape remind her of the *Arabian Nights,* and *King Lear,* and the Bible.

Against this backdrop of artifice and literature the figures of the natives stand out, and it is the picture of the natives that is the most significant for our present purpose. They possess so many of the qualities and beliefs that the figures in the tales exhibit. As in the tales Dinesen uses metaphors to suggest significant likenesses between people and animals, and as in the tales this is done for the purpose of esthetic distance as well as for comic effect, not in order to suggest significant character traits.

Thus Kamante is compared to "a dark bat that had strayed into the room, with very big spreading ears, or like a small African Will-o'-the-wisp, with his lamp in his hand" (OA, p. 40). Dinesen herself is a "lioness" (OA, p. 70). Three Kikuyus are compared to "three dirty and shaggy old Hyenas" and to "three ticks upon a sheep" (OA, p. 118). The young Masai warriors have neck muscles that "swell in a particular sinister fashion, like the neck of the angry cobra, the male leopard or the fighting bull" (OA, p. 135). The chief Kinanjui has a nose like "the trunk of an elephant . . . it was both boldly inquisitive and extremely sensitive and prudent, intensely on the offensive and on the defensive as well" (OA, p. 145). The old native women have gapes "like crocodiles" (OA, p. 165). A mother has "an impressive figure, very stout, with the powerful and benevolent placidity of a female elephant" (OA, p. 177). The young Somali women are like "three ferocious young she-wolves in seemly sheep's clothing" (OA, p. 179). Farah's son is compared to "a small falcon on your hand, a lion-cub on the knee" (OA, p. 186). The natives are often compared to elephants:

> The old dark clear-eyed Native of Africa, and the old dark clear-eyed Elephant,—they are alike; you see them standing on the ground, weighty with such impressions of the world around them as have been slowly gathered and heaped up in their dim minds; they are themselves features of the land [OA, p. 377].

Some of the old women have "the silhouette of a prehistoric animal, or a Giraffe" (OA, p. 385). An old woman breaks into tears without a word, "tears streaming over her face, like a cow that makes water on the plain before you" (OA, p. 385).

Having seen that the African setting, the landscape, the flora and fauna, and the human beings are rendered in a manner similar, if not identical, to that of the tales, we are not surprised when we realize that Dinesen has invested the natives with many of the character traits that we have observed among the heroes and heroines of the tales. Like many of the figures in the tales the natives in *Out of Africa* appear as aristocrats, full of pride and dignity, and on friendly terms with destiny. They appear as artists of the mask, possessing a fine imagination. They appear as marionette figures, regarding life as a ritual. They appear as figures who recognize their utter dependence on an arbitrary God, yet they possess a religion of acceptance and affirmation. Thus the same motifs that we saw running through the tales appear in *Out of Africa,* and the same underlying structure of values is basic to both. It was in Africa that Dinesen's world obtained its formal and ideological structure, the world which was later to be embodied in the tales. In the formation of this world the natives played a large role. "From my first weeks in Africa," says Dinesen,

> I had felt a great affection for the Natives. It was a strong feeling that embraced all ages and both sexes. The discovery of the dark races was to me a magnificent enlargement of all my world. If a person with an inborn sympathy for animals had grown up in a milieu where there were no animals, and had come into contact with animals late in life; or if a person with an instinctive taste for woods and forest had entered a forest for the first time at the age of twenty; or if some one with an ear for music had happened to hear music for the first time when he was already grown up; their cases might have been similar to mine. After I had met with the Natives, I set out the routine of my daily life to the Orchestra [OA, pp. 17-18].

And yet, she says, "When I was a young girl it was very far from my thoughts to go to Africa, nor did I dream then that an African farm should be the place in which I should be perfectly happy. That goes to prove that God has a greater and finer power of imagination than we have."

Many of the natives appear as true aristocrats. This is the case with the Masai in particular. "A Masai warrior," says Dinesen,

> is a fine sight. Those young men have, to the utmost extent, that particular form of intelligence which we call *chic*;—daring, and wildly fantastical as they seem, they are still unswervingly true to their own nature, and to an immanent ideal. Their style is not an assumed manner, nor an imitation of a foreign perfection, it has grown from inside, and is an expression of the race and its history, and their weapons and finery are as much part of their being as are a stag's antlers [OA, p. 135].

When put in prison they die within three months because they have a "stark inability to keep alive under the yoke," and this has given them a rank "with the immigrant aristocracy" (OA, p. 148).

But other natives besides the Masai are aristocratic. The Somali women are described as having "dignified, gentle ways, and were hospitable and gay, with a laughter like silver bells" (OA, p. 12). Her servant Farah's women are said to be "the glass of fashion and the mould of maidenly form. Indeed, here were three young women of the most exquisite dignity and demureness; I have never known ladies more ladylike" (OA, pp. 176-77).

One quality which the natives possess in abundance is courage: "They had real courage," says Dinesen, "the un-adulterated liking of danger" (OA, p. 24). They are coura-geous because they are "adjusted for the unforeseen and accustomed to the unexpected" (OA, p. 23). In this respect, says Dinesen, they differ from most white men, "of whom the majority strive to insure themselves against the unknown and the assaults of fate" (OA, p. 23). The native is "on friendly terms with destiny, having been in her hands all his time; she is to him, in a way, his home, the familiar darkness of the hut, deep mould for his roots. He faces any change in life with great calm" (OA, p. 23).

Many natives are praised for other aristocratic virtues. Thus the old chief Kinanjui shows "much originality of mind, and a rich, daring, imaginative spirit" (OA, p. 142). His death is one of the moving scenes in *Out of Africa,* and reveals Dinesen's sense of the old chief's greatness as well as her own high regard for life and death conceived as a dignified ritual (OA, p. 333).

The same high regard for the ritualistic aspects of existence is evinced in the description of the marriage customs of the Somalis. The Somali system, with its bartering, appeals to Dinesen because it helps her to understand

> . . . how my grandfather and great-grandfather were forced to their knees. The Somali system was at once a natural necessity and a fine art, it was both religion, strategy, and ballet, and was practiced in all respects with due devotion, discipline and dexterity. The great sweetness of it lay in the play of opposite forces within it. Behind the eternal principle of refutation, there was much generosity; behind the pedantry what risibility, and contempt of death. These daughters of a fighting race went through their ceremonial of primness as through a great graceful war-dance; butter would not melt in their mouth, neither would they rest till they had drunk their heart's blood of their adversary, they figured like three ferocious young she-wolves in seemly sheep's clothing [OA, p. 179].

Among the qualities that the natives value very highly is imagination. A master is great because he has a fine imagination; God is great because He has the finest imagination.

It may be on the strength of such a taste, that the Caliph Haroun al Raschid maintains, to the hearts of Africa and Arabia, his position as an ideal ruler; with him nobody knew what to expect next, and you did not know where you had him. When the Africans speak of the personality of God they speak like the Arabian Nights or like the last chapters of the book of Job; it is the same quality, the infinite power of imagination, with which they are impressed [OA, p. 23].

They have a deep dislike of "regularity, or any repeated treatment of the systematization of the whole" (OA, p. 24).

Thus we might say about the natives that they like a master or a God who is a bit of an actor, an artist of the mask, since what they dislike is repetition. Dinesen even suggests that what the natives fear the most from white men is "pedantry": "In the hands of a pedant they die of grief" (OA, p. 24). The natives live, like the artists of the mask, in a world in which anything is possible. One night after midnight Dinesen was awakened by her servant Kamante who told her he thought she had better get up because, he said, "I think that God is coming." When she got up he took her to the window and in the west she saw a big grass fire. When seen from the house it looked, says Dinesen, "as if some gigantic figure was moving and coming towards us." She explained the situation to Kamante, but he still persisted: "Well, yes, it may be so. But I thought you had better get up in case it was God coming" (OA, p. 41).

Since the natives value imagination in a master and in a god, it is not surprising that they value the Book of Job. The God of the Book of Job is the all-powerful God whose imagination transcends human comprehension and against whom it is foolish to rebel. From this God anything might be expected: He cannot be appeased if He is angry, or cajoled into doing man's will. If He loves you, He may destroy you. If you

138

are good, He sends you afflictions. This God is arbitrary, He acts gratuitously. As a result the natives do not try to "insure themselves against the unknown and the assaults of fate" (OA, p. 23). They are without apprehension of any risk. They recognize their utter dependency on God. The Book of Job is similar in spirit to the native conception of God in that it is not defending the greatness of God on the basis of His being a just God. Justice does not enter into the picture. What matters is the recognition that God's power and imagination transcend all understanding. This also means that God is not necessarily a good God, but that God and the Devil might, in effect, be one and the same person. Commenting on the fact that the natives were "in life itself, within their own element, such as we can never be, like fishes in deep water which for the life of them cannot understand our fear of drowning," Dinesen attributes this assurance of the natives to the fact that "they had preserved a knowledge that was lost to us by our first parents; Africa, amongst the continents, will teach it to you: that God and the Devil are one, the majesty coeternal, not two uncreated but one uncreated, and the Natives neither confounded the persons nor divided the substance" (OA, pp. 19-20).

Out of Africa centers around Africa and the natives, but in addition it deals with some interesting individuals with whom Dinesen came into personal contact during her long stay in Kenya, and it relates the personal tragedy of Dinesen, the loss of the farm and the death of Denys, two events that must have played a large part in determining her own destiny and future course as a writer.

Many of the figures portrayed in Out of Africa are of interest because they are like some of the figures in the tales. There is, first of all, Emmanuelson, Swedish maître d'hôtel in Nairobi, but in reality an actor, a tragic actor, whose favorite parts were those of Armand in *La Dame aux Camélias* and of Oswald in *Ghosts*. Down and out, and a rather shabby sight, he could still identify the bouquet of a Chambertin 1906, and he was, though a proletarian, a true aristocrat. His great feat was in crossing a desert on his way to Tanganyika, without water, and going through very dangerous lion territory. He was saved by the fact that the Masai found him on the road and took him in and let him travel with them in return for his entertaining them (by means of pantomime!) with accounts of his adventures in many countries.

The picture of Emmanuelson is drawn with sympathy. When Emmanuelson left the farm on his long trek across the desert, "I felt," says Dinesen, "my heart filling with the love and gratitude which the people who stay at home are feeling for the wayfarers and wanderers of the world, the sailors, explorers and vagabonds" (OA, p. 202). After learning of his being taken care of by the Masai, she considers it fit and becoming that this should have been so, because

> the true aristocracy and the true proletariat of the world are both in understanding with tragedy. To them it is the fundamental principle of God, and the key,—the minor key,—to existence. They differ in this way from the bourgeoisie of all classes, who deny tragedy, who will not tolerate it, and to whom the world of tragedy means in itself unpleasantness. Many misunderstandings between the white middleclass immigrant settlers and the Natives arise from this fact. The sulky Masai are both aristocracy and proletariat, they would have recognized at once in the lonely wanderer in black, a figure of tragedy; and the tragic actor had come, with them, into his own [OA, p. 204].

Emmanuelson had also a religion with which Dinesen must have felt a certain affinity: "Perhaps you will think me a terrible sceptic," said Emmanuelson, "if I now say what I am going to say. But with the exception of God I believe in absolutely nothing whatever" (OA, p. 201). It need hardly be pointed out that Emmanuelson is a figure very similar to that of Kasparson in "The Deluge at Norderney."

Like Emmanuelson, the rest of the figures are all colorful personalities. There is Hugh Martin, a civil servant, who looked "like an immensely fat Chinese Idol," and referred to Dinesen as Candide, and "was himself a curious Doctor Pangloss of the farm, firmly and placidly rooted in his conviction of the meanness and contemptibleness of human nature and of the Universe, and content in his faith, for why should it not be so?" (OA, p. 207). There is Charles Bulpett of Nairobi, a great friend of Dinesen who, she says, "was a kind of ideal to me, the English gentleman of the Victorian age, and quite at home in our own. He had swum the Hellespont, and had been one of the first to climb the Matterhorn, and he had been, in his early youth, in the 'eighties perhaps, La Belle Otero's lover," and felt it was worthwhile to have spent a hundred thousand for her sake in six months (OA, p. 210). He was a great traveler: "he had been all over the world and had tasted everywhere the best it had to offer, and he had not cared to secure his future so long as he could enjoy the present moment" (OA, p. 39).

There is Old Knudsen, the blind old Dane, with "the soul of a berserk," who always spoke of his great exploits in the third person in order to impose a mighty figure on the listener's mind and obscure the real, bent old man: "This little, humble man had made it his mission in life to uphold and extol the name of Old Knudsen, even to death. For he had really seen Old Knudsen, which nobody else except God ever had, and after that he would stand no heresy in anyone" (OA, pp. 58-59).

Then there are the two wanderers and dreamers, Berkeley Cole and Denys Finch-Hatton, both English immigrants, both "outcasts":

It was not a society that had thrown them out, and not any place in the whole world either, but time had done it, they did not belong to their century. No other nation than the English could have produced them, but they were examples of atavism, and theirs was an earlier England, a world which no longer existed. In the present epoch they had no home, but had got to wander here and there, and in the course of time they also came to the farm [OA, p. 213].

Berkeley, says Dinesen, might have been a cavalier of the Court of King Charles II, and he was a great jester and buffoon. He was like a cat in that the law of gravitation did not seem to apply to him; all about him was "a presence of gracefulness, gaiety and freedom," and for this reason his death was a great loss to the colony. "As Berkeley went away, a grim figure made her entrance upon the stage from the opposite wing,—*la dure necessité, maîtresse des hommes et des dieux*" (OA, p. 224).

Denys Finch-Hatton was also an exile for he "could indeed have been placed harmoniously in any period of our civilization, *tout comme chez soi*, all up till the opening of the nineteenth century" (OA, p. 215). He was an athlete, a musician, an art lover, and a fine sportsman. He lived on the farm between his safaris because he had no other home, and there was undoubtedly a strong atachment between Dinesen and Denys Hatton. Denys, says Dinesen, gave her the "greatest, the most transporting pleasure" of her life when he allowed her to fly with him over Africa (OA, p. 237). His death in a plane accident was a great loss to Dinesen, and the account of his death and his funeral is the most moving chapter in the book. Denys was a true aristocrat, and it came as no surprise to Dinesen to hear some years after she had left Africa that lions were seen standing or lying on his grave: "It was fit and decorous that the lions should come to Denys' grave and make him an African monument . . . Lord Nelson himself, I have reflected, in Trafalgar Square, has lions made only out of stone" (OA, pp. 360-61).

Denys Hatton's death was a tragedy, and so was the loss of the farm. The latter part of *Out of Africa* relates this tragic loss: how drought, grasshoppers, fevers, coffee diseases, and falling coffee prices conspired to this end. This experience must have brought to Dinesen a deep understanding of the native religion. When the rains did not materialize, then you realized your utter dependency on God, she says. All the afflictions which she was to suffer must have appeared to her as the afflictions of Job, heaped upon her by malicious powers. Sometimes she felt like the man in the story about the stork: like a blind person, or an animal in the zoo, or a marionette (OA, pp. 251-53).

Her servants, the Kikuyus, accepted the situation with much greater case "on account of their superior inside knowledge of God and the Devil" (OA, p. 331). But Dinesen looked for some "central principle" within what was happening: "All this could not be, I thought, just a coincidence of circumstances, what people call a run of bad luck." She looked for a sign, a sign that would make "the coherence of things" clear to her (OA, p. 368).

She received the sign. Walking toward the boys' huts, she saw a scene that left her frightened, "such a dangerous place did the world seem to me." What she saw was a gruesome scene in which a big white cock walked straight up to a little gray chameleon that happened to be very brave and opened his mouth and stuck out his tongue to mock his enemy, whereupon the cock struck down his beak and plucked out the chameleon's tongue. How was this sign to be interpreted? Dinesen felt that she had received "the most spiritual answer possible," and that she had been

... in a strange manner honoured and distinguished. The powers to which I had cried had stood on my dignity more than I had done myself, and what other answer could they then give? This was clearly not the hour for coddling, and they had chosen to connive at my invocation of it. Great powers had laughed to me, with an echo from the hills to follow the laughter, they had said among the trumpets, among the cocks and Chameleons, Ha ha! [OA, pp. 369-70].

This interpretation is not perfectly clear. It seems to indicate three different things. First, that things happen that are beyond our imagination; second, that God and the Devil are the same power; and third, that the heavenly powers can only be defied proudly, with laughter and courage.

On the last day, says Dinesen, the day

... on which I was going away, I learned the strange learning that things can happen which we ourselves cannot possibly imagine, either beforehand, or at the time when they are taking place, or afterwards when we look back on them. Circumstances can have a motive force by which they bring about events without aid of human imagination or apprehension. On such occasions you yourself keep in touch with what is going on by attentively following it from moment to moment, like a blind person who is being led, and who places one foot in front of the other cautiously but unwittingly. Things are happening to you, and you feel them happening, but except for this one fact you have no connection with them, and no key to the cause or meaning of them. The performing wild animals in a circus go through their programme, I believe, in that same way. Those who have been through such events can, in a way, say that they have been through death—a passage outside the range of imagination, but within the range of experience [OA, pp. 385-86].

What Dinesen describes here is the tragic recognition as such; it is the recognition of Job, of Oedipus, of King Lear. It is no accident that the name of Lear appears so often on the last pages of *Out of Africa*, for Lear attains this final awareness as well at the close of his tragedy, after having been a victim of the same kind of experience, a feeling that all events have lost their rhyme or reason.

The tragedy of Lear also expresses an idea which Dinesen seems to have in mind at this point: the idea expressed by Edgar (who, according to Dinesen, speaks for Shakespeare) that the gods make sport of us, that they are malicious, and that we are as flies to them.[5] Dinesen's little story of the chameleon seems to suggest that the gods are perfectly capable of being malicious.

But if the gods and the devils laugh at us the lesson from the story seems to be that we must laugh back at them. This is what the chameleon does. There is no use in appealing to the gods. This idea is also expressed in "The Deluge at Norderney." At the end of the story Kasparson says:

> For I have lived long enough, by now, to have learned, when the devil grins at me, to grin back. And what now if this—to grin back when the devil grins at you—be in reality the highest, the only true fun in all the world? And what if everything else, which people have named fun, be only a presentiment, a foreshadowing, of it? It is an art worth learning, then [SGT, pp. 77-78].

To which Miss Nat-og-Dag answers: "I have grinned back at him too. It is an art worth learning."

Isak Dinesen was to learn how to grin back at the Devil. The chameleon used his tongue, she used the instrument of the tongue, the pen.

Thus it came about that three years after her return from Africa, in 1934, Isak Dinesen published *Seven Gothic Tales* and began, in defiance of the gods, to recreate in her tales the world she had lost. Finding herself, like her father, many years before, divorced from a life of excitement and adventure, she began writing stories which would take her mind and thoughts away to past times and exotic lands.[6]

NOTES

Introduction

1. Dorothy Canfield, "Introduction," *Seven Gothic Tales* (New York: The Modern Library, 1934), p. vi.
2. George Davis has called my attention to H. C. Andersen's references to Adolph Wilhelm Dinesen in his Roman Journals.
3. See Gunnar Unger, "På thé hos baronessan," *Svenska Dagbladet*, March 3, 1957, p. 7.
4. Hans Brix, *Karen Blixens Eventyr* (Copenhagen: Gyldendal, 1949), pp. 231-58.
5. Eugene Walter, "The Art of Fiction: Isak Dinesen," *Paris Review*, Autumn, 1956, pp. 47-48.
6. Tom Kristensen, "Syv fantastiske Fortaellinger," *Mellem Krigene* (Copenhagen: Gyldendal, 1946), pp. 134-40.
7. Cf. Sven Møller Kristensen, *Dansk Litteratur 1918-1950* (Copenhagen: E. Munksgaard, 1951), p. 20; P. M. Mitchell, *A History of Danish Literature* (Copenhagen: Gyldendal, 1957), p. 275; and Emil Fredriksen, *Ung Dansk Litteratur 1930-1950* (Copenhagen: Schønberg, 1951), p. 7.
8. See Gunnar Brandell, "Nittiotalets berättare," *Ny Illustrerad Svensk Litteraturhistoria*, ed. E. N. Tigerstedt (Stockholm: Natur och Kultur, 1952-57), IV, 318.
9. Kristensen, *Dansk Litteratur 1918-1950*, p. 20.

10. P. M. Mitchell has entitled one of the chapters in his book "A Need for Myth: Danish Literature since 1940," *A History of Danish Literature,* pp. 279 ff.

11. This new trend toward storytelling and fantasy might be seen in the works of the Danish writers Frank Jaeger, Willy-August Linnemann, and Eiler Jørgensen, or in the novels of the young Swedish writer Per Wästberg. See Bibliography.

Chapter 1

1. Walter, "The Art of Fiction: Isak Dinesen," p. 58.
2. Brix, *Karen Blixens Eventyr,* p. 16.
3. See Joseph Campbell's introduction to *The Portable Arabian Nights* (New York: The Viking Press, 1952), pp. 1-2.
4. These are some of the works and authors listed by Dinesen as appealing to her. See Walter, "The Art of Fiction: Isak Dinesen," p. 57.
5. Lionel Trilling, "The Story and the Novel," *The Griffin,* VII (January, 1958), 8.
6. *Ibid.,* p. 7.
7. W. H. Auden, "Reflections on Music and Opera," *Partisan Review,* XIX (January-February, 1952). The following page references in the text are to this essay.
8. Morton Dauwen Zabel, *Craft and Character in Modern Fiction* (New York: The Viking Press, 1957), p. 150.
9. *Ibid.,* p. 147.
10. Trilling, "The Story and the Novel," p. 5.
11. Walter, "The Art of Fiction: Isak Dinesen," p. 58.
12. Cf. the English novelist Iris Murdoch writing about Jean Paul Sartre and the modern novel: "The modern novelist is not usually telling us about events as if they were past and remembered; he is presenting them, through the consciousness of his people, as if they were happening now. . . . This method has both its peculiar appropriateness to the present time (we are not now so anxious to regard minds as *things* which can be adequately described from the outside, or from a distance), and also its pe-

culiar difficulties." *Sartre, Romantic Rationalist* (New Haven: Yale University Press, 1953), p. 37.

13. Staffan Björck, "Kardinal Dinesen berättar," *Dagens Nyheter*, November 4, 1957, p. 4.

14. Eino Railo, *The Haunted Castle* (London: E. P. Dutton and Co., 1927), p. 315.

15. Christian Elling, "Karen Blixen," *Danske Digtere i det Tyvende Aarhundrede*, ed. Ernst Frandsen and Niels Kaas Johansen (Copenhagen: G. E. C. Gad, 1951), p. 540.

16. Brix, *Karen Blixens Eventyr*, p. 144.

17. Elling, "Karen Blixen," pp. 537-38.

18. *Ibid.*, p. 542.

19. Karen Blixen, *En Baaltale med 14 Aars Forsinkelse* (Copenhagen: Berlingske forlag, 1954). The following references in the text are to this speech.

20. Elling, "Karen Blixen," p. 547.

21. Robert Louis Stevenson, "Olalla," *The Novels and Tales*, (New York: Charles Scribner's Sons, 1911), VII, 142 ff.

22. Pär Lagerkvist, *Barabbas* (New York: Random House, 1951), p. 3.

23. Walter, "The Art of Fiction: Isak Dinesen," pp. 56-58.

24. Jørgen Gustava Brandt, "Et Essay om Karen Blixen," *Heretica*, VI (1953), 313.

25. William G. O'Donnell, "Kierkegaard: The Literary Manner," *Kenyon Review*, IX (Winter, 1947), 43-44.

26. Karen Blixen, "Breve fra et Land i Krig," *Dansk Skrivekunst*, ed. Erling Nielsen (Oslo: J. W. Cappelens, 1955), p. 20.

Chapter 2

1. Paul la Cour, "Fantasi og Virkelighed," *Tilskueren*, November, 1935, pp. 336-42.

2. Harald Nielsen, *Karen Blixen: En Studie i litteraer Mystik* (Copenhagen: Borgen, 1956), p. 62, pp. 93-110.

3. In *The Romantic Agony* (New York: Oxford University

Press, 1956), Mario Praz combines the Gothic and the Decadent movements.

4. Holbrook Jackson, *The Eighteen Nineties* (London: Pelican Books, 1939), p. 62.

5. Pierre Andrézel, *The Angelic Avengers* (New York: Random House, 1947), p. 147. Two of Dinesen's most recent tales, "The Diver," and "Tempests," also describe men and women who wish to escape from their limitations.

6. Praz, *The Romantic Agony*, p. 314.

7. Brix, *Karen Blixens Eventyr*, pp. 231 ff.

Chapter 3

1. Cf. the descriptions of Dinesen's appearance in the *Paris Review* interview, p. 45. Eugene Walter also feels that the suggestion put forth a few years ago that Greta Garbo was to play Dinesen in a film based on *Out of Africa* was excellent "typecasting" (p. 43).

2. *Ibid.*, p. 57.

3. William Butler Yeats, *Essays* (New York: The Macmillan Co., 1924), p. 496.

4. In early stories like *Tonio Kröger* and later novels such as *Felix Krull, Confidence Man.*

Chapter 4

1. Nielsen, *Karen Blixen: En Studie i litteraer Mystik,* pp. 62-65, and Aage Henriksen, *Karen Blixen og Marionetterne* (Copenhagen: Wivel, 1952).

2. Karen Blixen-Finecke, "Sandhedens Haevn," *Tilskueren,* May, 1926, pp. 329-44.

3. Henriksen, *Karen Blixen og Marionetterne,* pp. 20-21.

4. *Ibid.*, pp. 10-11.

5. *Ibid.*, pp. 51 ff.

6. Hjalmar Bergman (1882-1931) was, like Isak Dinesen, interested in the *Arabian Nights,* some of which he translated; he

has written sagas and fairy tales; his works demonstrate a preoccupation with mask and marionette (he wrote several marionette plays); and his themes often center around the conception of life as adventure in contrast to the dullness and respectability of middle-class existence. See Per Lindberg, *Bakom masker* (Stockholm: Bonnier, 1949), pp. 55-152.

7. Thomas Genelli has called my attention to Joseph Conrad's interest in marionettes. In a letter to R. B. Cunninghame Graham of December 6, 1897, Conrad writes: "But I love a marionette-show. Marionettes are beautiful—especially those of the old kind with wires, thick as my little finger, coming out of the top of the head. Their impassibility in love, in crime, in mirth, in sorrow,— is heroic, superhuman, fascinating. Their rigid violence when they fall upon one another to embrace or to fight is simply a joy to behold. I never listen to the text mouthed somewhere out of sight by invisible men who are here today and rotten tomorrow. I love the marionettes that are without life, that come so near to being immortal!" See G. Jean-Aubry, *Joseph Conrad, Life and Letters* (New York: Doubleday, Page and Co., 1927), I, 213.

Chapter 5

1. Karen Blixen, *Farah* (Copenhagen: Wivel, 1950). The following references in the text are to this work.

2. Thomas Dinesen also published a book about his war experiences, *Merry Hell!* (London: Jarrolds, Ltd., [1930]). He is also a writer of short stories, collected in *Syrenbusken* (Copenhagen: Jespersen og Pio, 1951).

3. Georg Brandes, "Wilhelm Dinesen," *Samlede Skrifter* (Copenhagen: Gyldendal, 1900), III, 203-17.

4. Boganis, *Jagtbreve* (Copenhagen: Gyldendal, 1949).

5. Brandes, "Wilhelm Dinesen," p. 206.

6. Boganis, *Jagtbreve*, pp. 60-61.

7. In Scandinavian literature the Swedish poet, novelist, and essayist Frans G. Bengtsson—author of *The Long Ships*, trans. Michael Meyer (London: Collins, 1954), a pastiche of the Ice-

landic saga, and *Karl XII:s levnad* (Stockholm: Norstedt, 1954), a tribute to the noble and aristocratic Swedish King—is perhaps the writer closest to Dinesen's aristocratic outlook on life.

8. See Morton Dauwen Zabel's introduction to *The Portable Conrad* (New York: The Viking Press, 1947), p. 14.

9. Joseph Conrad, *Lord Jim* (New York: Doubleday and Co., 1920), p. 214.

10. Zabel, *The Portable Conrad*, pp. 2-3.

11. Dinesen's idea of nemesis is, as Johannes Rosendahl has pointed out, related to Meir Aron Goldschmidt's (1819-87). Cf. *Karen Blixen, Fire Foredrag* (Copenhagen: Gyldendal, 1957), pp. 27-29.

12. Elling, "Karen Blixen," p. 527.

13. "Sorrow Acre" is an example of Dinesen's use of folk-tale motifs. Her story is based on Paul la Cour's retelling of this old folk tale in "Danske Sagaer," *Tilskueren*, March, 1931, pp. 231-40.

14. Cf. the heroes of Alfred de Vigny who have faith in honor and nothing else. *The Military Necessity*, trans. Humphrey Hare (London: Cresset Press, 1953), p. 205.

15. *Farah*, pp. 5-7.

16. *En Baaltale*, p. 14.

17. Brandt, "Et Essay om Karen Blixen," p. 209.

Chapter 6

1. See Ernst Frandsen's introduction to *Danske Digtere i det Tyvende Aarhundrede*, ed. Ernst Frandsen and Niels Kaas Johansen (Copenhagen: G. E. C. Gad, 1951), p. 21.

2. Brandt, "Et Essay om Karen Blixen," p. 303.

3. Albert Camus, *The Rebel* (New York: Vintage Books, 1956), pp. 23-25. Cf. also my article, "Pär Lagerkvist and the Art of Rebellion," *Scandinavian Studies*, XXX (February, 1958), 19-29.

4. Brandt, "Et Essay om Karen Blixen," p. 208.

5. *Ibid.*, p. 304.

6. Cf. Joseph Conrad's remarks in *A Personal Record*: "The

ethical view of the universe involves us at last in so many cruel and absurd contradictions, where the last vestiges of faith, hope, charity, and even of reason itself, seem ready to perish, that I have come to suspect that the aim of creation cannot be ethical at all. I would fondly believe that its object is purely spectacular; a spectacle for awe, love, adoration, or hate, if you like, but in this view—and in this view alone—never for despair!" Quoted in *The Portable Conrad,* pp. 712-13.

7. Børge Gedsø Madsen, "Karen Blixen: Kardinalens Tredie Historie," *Scandinavian Studies,* XXVI (May, 1954), 103.

Chapter 7

1. Mitchell, *A History of Danish Literature,* p. 276, comments on *Out of Africa* as being "seemingly incompatible with the fantastic literature of her pseudonyms," and on "the discrepancy between the literature of phantasy and the interpretation of a primitive culture."

2. Nielsen, *Karen Blixen: En Studie i litteraer Mystik,* pp. 20-21.

3. Walter, "The Art of Fiction: Isak Dinesen," p. 51.

4. Dinesen's descriptions of the self-contained worlds of animals, people, and things resemble Rainer Maria Rilke's poems from the Rodin period. Cf. the self-sufficiency and self-absorption of Rilke's animals ("Die Flamingos," for instance), living within a world of their own, without any need of the outside world.

5. Karen Blixen, "Breve fra et Land i Krig," *Dansk Skrivekunst,* ed. Erling Nielsen (Oslo: J. W. Cappelens, 1955), p. 28.

6. *Shadows on the Grass,* which was published after this study was already in press, contains four reminiscences about the decade when Dinesen ran a coffee plantation in Kenya. The most significant of these pieces, the portrait of Farah, her faithful Somali major-domo, I have discussed in the chapter on "Aristocracy," since it was printed in Danish in 1950.

The other recollections are written in the elegiac but unsentimental tone of *Out of Africa,* though they lack the formal perfection of the earlier work. In "Barua a Soldani" and "The Great Gesture" Dinesen tells of her experiences as a doctor to the squatters on the farm, experiences which are both amusing and touching. "Echoes from the Hills" relates of the further adventures of Farah, Kamante, Old Knudsen, and other familiar figures from *Out of Africa.*

The volume contains three sensitive portraits by the author.

BIBLIOGRAPHY

The Works of Isak Dinesen

In Danish

"Eneboerne," *Tilskueren*, August, 1907, pp. 609-35.

"Pløjeren," *Gads Danske Magasin*, October, 1907, pp. 50-59.

"Sandsynlige Historier. Familien de Cats," *Tilskueren*, January, 1909, pp. 1-19.

"Ex Africa," *Tilskueren*, April, 1925, pp. 244-46.

"Sandhedens Haevn," *Tilskueren*, May, 1926, pp. 329-44.

Syv fantastiske Fortaellinger. Copenhagen: Reitzel, 1935.

Den afrikanske Farm. Copenhagen: Gyldendal, 1937.

"Karyatiderne," *Tilskueren*, April, 1938, pp. 269-308. (Reprinted in *Sidste Fortaellinger*. Copenhagen: Gyldendal, 1957.)

Vintereventyr. Copenhagen: Gyldendal, 1942.

Gengaeldelsens Veje, trans. Clara Svendsen. Copenhagen: Gyldendal, 1944.

"Breve fra et Land i Krig," *Heretica*, I (1948), 264-87, 332-55. (Reprinted in *Dansk Skrivekunst*, ed. Erling Nielsen. Oslo: J. W. Cappelens, 1955, pp. 1-34.)

Om Retskrivning. Copenhagen: Gyldendal, 1949.

Farah. Copenhagen: Wivel, 1950.

Daguerreotypier. Copenhagen: Gyldendal, 1951.

Kardinalens Tredie Historie. Et grafisk vaerk ved Erik Clemmensen. Copenhagen: Gyldendal, 1952.
"Samtale om Natten i København," *Heretica,* VI (1953), 465-94. (Reprinted in *Sidste Fortaellinger.* Copenhagen: Gyldendal, 1957.)
En Baaltale med 14 Aars Forsinkelse. Copenhagen: Berlingske forlag, 1954.
"Dykkeren," *Vindrosen,* I (November, 1954), 400-14.
Babettes Gaestebud. Copenhagen: Forlaget Fremad, 1955.
Spøgelsehestene. Copenhagen: Forlaget Fremad, 1955.
Sidste Fortaellinger. Copenhagen: Gyldendal, 1957.
"H. C. Branner: Rytteren," *Bazar,* April, 1958, pp. 51-63; May, 1958, pp. 71-94.
Skaebne-Anekdoter. Copenhagen: Gyldendal, 1958.

In English

Seven Gothic Tales. New York: The Modern Library, 1934.
Out of Africa. New York: Random House, 1938.
Winter's Tales. New York: Random House, 1942.
The Angelic Avengers. New York: Random House, 1946.
"Uncertain Heiress," *Saturday Evening Post,* CCXXII (December 10, 1949), 34 ff.
"Babette's Feast," *Ladies Home Journal,* LXVII (June, 1950), 34 ff. (Reprinted in *Anecdotes of Destiny.*)
"Ghost Horses," *Ladies Home Journal,* LXVIII (October, 1951), 56 ff.
"The Immortal Story," *Ladies Home Journal,* LXX (February, 1953), 34 ff. (Reprinted in *Anecdotes of Destiny.*)
"The Cloak," *Ladies Home Journal,* LXXII (May, 1955), 52 ff. (Reprinted in *Last Tales.*)
"The Caryatids," *Ladies Home Journal,* LXXIV (November, 1957), 64 ff. (Reprinted in *Last Tales.*)
"Echoes," *Atlantic Monthly,* CC (November, 1957), 96-100. (Reprinted in *Last Tales.*)
Last Tales. New York: Random House, 1957.

Anecdotes of Destiny. New York: Random House, 1958.
Shadows on the Grass. New York: Random House, 1961.

OTHER WORKS CONSULTED

Auden, W. H. "Some Reflections on Music and Drama," *Partisan Review,* XIX (January-February, 1952), 10-18.

Barbey d'Aurevilly, Jules. *The Diaboliques,* trans. Ernest Boyd. New York: A. A. Knopf, 1925.

Bengtsson, Frans G. *Karl XII:s levnad.* 2 vols. Stockholm: Norstedt, 1935-36.

Berendsohn, Walter A. *Selma Lagerlöf.* Stockholm: Bonnier, 1928.

Bergman, Hjalmar. *Samlade Skrifter,* IX. Stockholm: Bonnier, 1949.

Björck, Staffan. "Kardinal Dinesen berättar," *Dagens Nyheter* (November 4, 1957), p. 4.

Boganis (pseudonym of Wilhelm Dinesen). *Jagtbreve.* Copenhagen: Gyldendal, 1949.

The Book of the Thousand Nights and One Night, trans. J. C. Mardrus. Rendered into English by Powys Mathers. 4 vols. London: C. Routledge, 1937.

Brandes, Georg. "Wilhelm Dinesen," *Samlede Skrifter,* III. Copenhagen: Gyldendal, 1900, pp. 203-17.

Brandt, Jørgen Gustava. "Et Essay om Karen Blixen," *Heretica,* VI (1953), 200-23, 300-20.

Brix, Hans. *Analyser og Problemer,* VI. Copenhagen: Gyldendal, 1950, pp. 286-305.

———. *Karen Blixens Eventyr.* Copenhagen: Gyldendal, 1949.

Campbell, Joseph, ed. *The Portable Arabian Nights.* New York: The Viking Press, 1952.

Castrén, Gunnar. "Den nya tiden," *Illustrerad Svensk Litteraturhistoria,* ed. Henrik Schück and Karl Warburg. Stockholm: Rabén och Sjögren, 1933.

Dinesen, Thomas. *Merry Hell!* London: Jarrolds, Ltd., [1930].

———. *Syrenbusken.* Copenhagen: Jespersen og Pio, 1951.

Elling, Christian. "Karen Blixen," *Danske Digtere i det Tyvende Aarhundrede,* ed. Ernst Frandsen and Niels Kaas Johansen. Copenhagen: G. E. C. Gad, 1951, pp. 521-71.

Frandsen, Ernst. "Udsigt over et halvt Aarhundrede," *Danske Digtere i det Tyvende Aarhundrede,* ed. Ernst Frandsen and Niels Kaas Johansen. Copenhagen: G. E. C. Gad, 1951, pp. 5-32.

Fredriksen, Emil. *Ung Dansk Litteratur 1930-1950.* Copenhagen: Schønberg, 1951.

Grandjean, Louis. *Blixens Animus.* Copenhagen: Grandjeans Publications Fond, 1957.

Henriksen, Aage. *Guder og Galgefugle.* Oslo: Det Norske studentersamfunds kulturutvalg, 1956.

————. *Karen Blixen og Marionetterne.* Copenhagen: Wivel, 1952.

Jackson, Holbrook. *The Eighteen Nineties.* London: Pelican Books, 1939.

Jaeger, Frank. *Hverdagshistorier.* Copenhagen: Wivel, 1951.

Jean-Aubry, G. *Joseph Conrad, Life and Letters.* 2 vols. New York: Doubleday, Page and Co., 1927.

Jørgensen, Eiler. *Mannen der huskede.* Copenhagen: Hasselbalch, 1951.

————. *Den lykkelige dal.* Copenhagen: Hasselbalch, 1952.

Kapel, Klaus Otto. "Karen Blixen: Skaebne-Anekdoter," *Vindrosen,* VI (January, 1959), 67-72.

Kehler, Henning. "Brev från Danmark," *Bonniers Litterära Magasin,* IV (December, 1935), 37-38.

Kierkegaard, Søren. *Stages on Life's Way,* trans. Walter Lowrie. Princeton: Princeton University Press, 1940.

Kristensen, Sven Møller. *Dansk Litteratur 1918-1950.* 2nd ed. Copenhagen: E. Munksgaard, 1951.

Kristensen, Tom. "Syv fantastiske Fortaellinger," *Mellem Krigene.* Copenhagen: Gyldendal, 1946, pp. 134-40.

————. "Karen Blixens nye, fantastiske Fortaellinger," *Til Dags Dato.* Copenhagen: Gyldendal, 1953, pp. 118-20.

la Cour, Paul. "Fantasi og Virkelighed," *Tilskueren*, November, 1935, pp. 336-42.

──────. "Danske Sagaer," *Tilskueren*, March, 1931, pp. 231-40.

Lange, Victor. "Deceptive Cadenza," *New Republic*, CXXXVII (November 18, 1957), 17-19.

Lindberg, Per. *Bakom masker*. Stockholm: Bonnier, 1949.

Linnemann, Willy-August. *Bogen om det skjulte Ansigt*. Copenhagen: Gyldendal, 1958.

Madsen, Børge G. "Isak Dinesen, a Modern Aristocrat," *American-Scandinavian Review*, XLI (December, 1953), 328-32.

──────. "Karen Blixen: Kardinalens Tredie Historie," *Scandinavian Studies*, XXVI (May, 1954), 101-3.

Mitchell, P. M. *A History of Danish Literature*. Copenhagen: Gyldendal, 1957.

Murdoch, Iris. *Sartre, Romantic Rationalist*. New Haven: Yale University Press, 1953.

Nielsen, Harald. *Karen Blixen: En Studie i litteraer Mystik*. Copenhagen: Borgen, 1956.

O'Donnell, William G. "Kierkegaard: The Literary Manner," *Kenyon Review*, IX (Winter, 1947), 35-47.

Railo, Eino. *The Haunted Castle*. London: E. P. Dutton and Co., 1927.

Riisager, Vagn. *Karen Blixen*. Copenhagen: Gyldendal, 1952.

Rosendahl, Johannes. *Karen Blixen: Fire Foredrag*. Copenhagen: Gyldendal, 1957.

Sandvad, Jørgen. "Jeg har altid vaeret forelsket," *Politiken*, October 27, 1957, pp. 23-24.

Stolpe, Sven. "Isak Dinesen under beskjutning," *Aftonbladet*, February 7, 1957, p. 2.

Trilling, Lionel. "The Story and the Novel," *The Griffin*, VII (January, 1958), 4-12.

Unger, Gunnar. "På thé hos baronessan," *Svenska Dagbladet*, March 3, 1957, p. 7.

Vigny, Alfred de. *The Military Necessity*, trans. Humphrey Hare. London: Cresset Press, 1943.

Wägner, Elin. *Selma Lagerlöf.* 2 vols. Stockholm: Bonnier, 1942.

Walter, Eugene. "The Art of Fiction: Isak Dinesen," *Paris Review,* Autumn, 1956, pp. 42-59.

Woel, Cai M. *Dansk Literaturhistorie 1900-1950,* II. [Odense]: Arnkrone, 1956.

Wästberg, Per. *Halva kungariket.* Stockholm: Wahlström och Widstrand, 1955.

Yeats, William Butler, *Autobiography.* New York: The Macmillan Co., 1953.

———. *Essays.* New York: The Macmillan Co., 1924.

Zabel, Morton Dauwen. *Craft and Character in Modern Fiction.* New York: The Viking Press, 1957.

———. *The Portable Conrad.* New York: The Viking Press, 1947.

INDEX